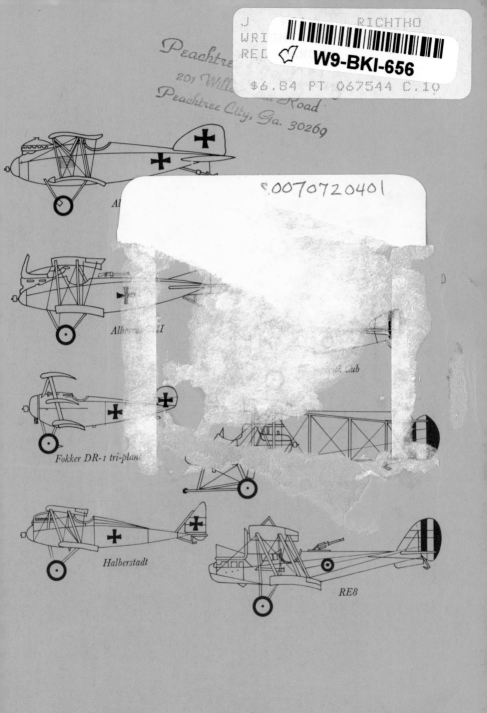

Al

Albatros II

Fokker DR-1 tri-plane

Halberstadt

RE8

The
Red
Baron

Nicolas Wright

The Red Baron

McGraw-Hill Book Company

New York   St. Louis   San Francisco

First published in Great Britain in 1976
by Sidgwick and Jackson Limited
1 Tavistock Chambers, Bloomsbury Way,
London WC1A 2SG.

Library of Congress Cataloging in Publication Data

Wright, Nicolas.
  The Red Baron.

  Includes index.
  SUMMARY: A biography of the World War I ace known as
the Red Baron who shot down 80 Allied planes before he
himself was killed, a month before his twenty-sixth birthday.
  1. Richthofen, Manfred Albrecht, Freiherr von, 1892–
1918—Juvenile literature. 2. Air pilots—Germany—Biography—Juvenile literature. 3. European War, 1914–1918
—Aerial operations, German—Juvenile literature. [1. Richthofen, Manfred Albrecht, Freiherr von, 1892–1918. 2. Air
pilots. 3. European War, 1914–1918—Aerial operations,
German] I. Title.
UG626.2.R5W74   940.4'49'430924 [B]   77-78759
ISBN 0-07-072040-1 lib. bdg.

First Distribution in the United States of America
by McGraw-Hill Inc., 1977.
Printed in the United States of America.

45 MUBP 789

For the Stocken children:
Jonathan, Simon, Claudia and Zebedee

Contents

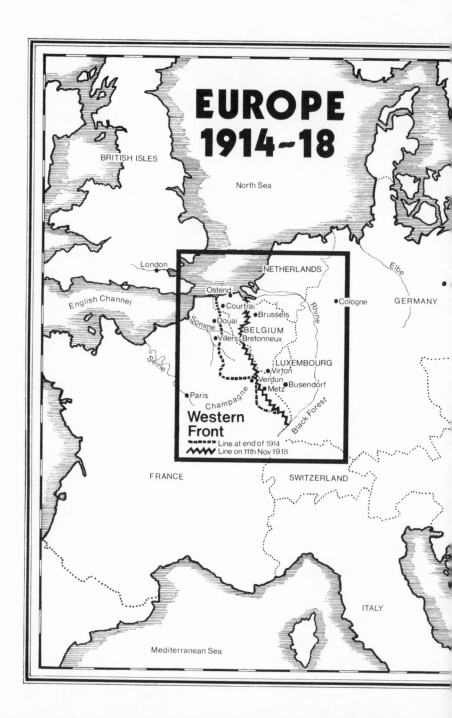

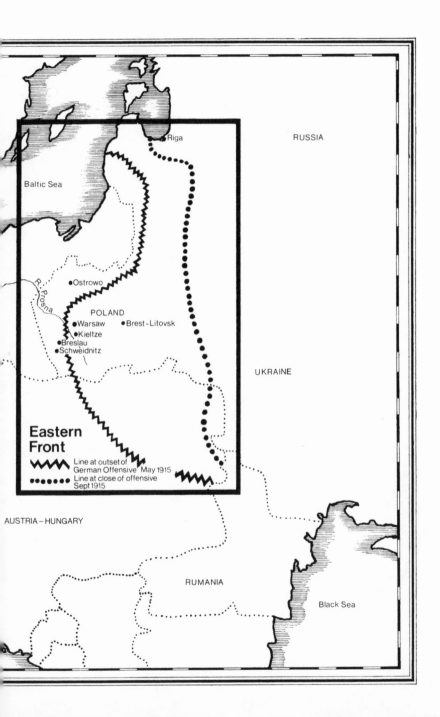

RUSSIA

Baltic Sea

Riga

R. Prosna

●Ostrowo

POLAND

●Warsaw   ●Brest-Litovsk
●Kieltze
●Breslau
●Schweidnitz

UKRAINE

**Eastern
Front**

〰〰〰 Line at outset of
German Offensive May 1915
●●●●●● Line at close of offensive
Sept 1915

AUSTRIA–HUNGARY

RUMANIA

Black Sea

Taken
on the Wing

For once Richthofen slept well and it was nearly eight o'clock before he awoke. As he dressed he glanced occasionally through the window. A low mist hung over the Cappy airfield but an already brightening sky promised sun later.

He was in a good mood. The day before he had shot down his eightieth enemy aircraft. There seemed no reason why today—April 21, 1918—he should not push his score even higher. He was also looking forward to the pleasant prospect of a hunting trip in the Black Forest, far away from the desolation of northern France.

After breakfast he stepped outside. Then his mood changed. For there, in front of his quarters, was a military band. The commander of a nearby division had arranged for it to play in honor of his latest victory. Richthofen, never a music lover, acknowledged the band only with a curt nod and walked off toward the hangars. As he did so he remarked to a companion that he found the music too loud.

Once at the hangars he soon regained his humor and happily agreed to autograph a postcard of himself for his mechanic's son.

"What's the matter?" he joked. "Don't you think I'll come back!"

He then inspected his aircraft, a Fokker DR-1 tri-plane. When he had finished he joined the other JG 1 pilots assigned to morning flying duty. They too were in high spirits and waited impatiently for a favorable weather report. Richthofen noticed that one of them, Lt. Richard Wenzl, a newcomer to the group, was dozing on a stretcher. Cautioning those watching to be quiet, he suddenly kicked the supports away. Everybody roared with laughter as the astonished Wenzl found himself deposited on the ground. He dusted his flying suit down and stalked off, pretending to be angry.

As soon as Wenzl was out of sight another pilot took his place on the stretcher. Richthofen ignored him for a few minutes and then, just as the unfortunate man was beginning to nod off, tipped him out too. The pilots were delighted. They had rarely seen their usually morose and taciturn leader in such a playful mood.

The second pilot hurried off to find Wenzl and together they tried to think of a way in which to get their own back. As they talked, Richthofen's dog, a Great Dane

1. A family group. Manfred von Richthofen (left), his uniform jacket festooned with medals, poses with his mother and father, his sister Ilse and the two younger Richthofen brothers, Lothar and Bolko.

2. Oswald Boelcke, the commanding officer of Jasta 2, Manfred von Richthofen's training ground as a fighter pilot. Boelcke shot down forty enemy aircraft before he was killed in an accidental midair collision with one of his own pupils.

3. Two great Richthofen aces. Manfred (right) and his high-scoring brother, Lothar.

4. While Manfred von Richthofen was recovering from a head wound received during an air battle, he was looked after by nurse Katie Otersdorf. It was rumored that they fell in love.

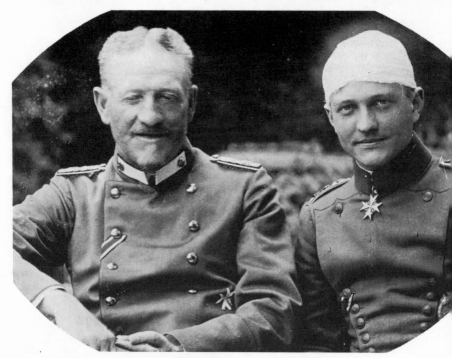

5. Above: *A welcome hospital visitor—Albrecht Baron von Richthofen, Manfred's father. The injured fighter was grounded for six weeks
following his lucky escape.*

6. Below: *Surrounded by other members of the famous Flying Circus,
Manfred von Richthofen admires the propeller from a British aircraft,
which they had brought to the hospital to cheer him up.*

called Moritz, wandered up. This was their chance. They seized him and tied a large, heavy wheel chock to his tail.

They doubled up as Moritz, not at all sure why he was being treated in such an unmannerly fashion, struggled off to find his master. Richthofen was checking his aircraft as he heard the dog's panting approach. When Moritz reached him and he saw what had happened, he smiled and released the animal. As Moritz jumped up gratefully to lick his master, Richthofen heard the click of a camera shutter.

Richthofen was furious. He looked around to see who had photographed him. He was a deeply superstitious man and never allowed pictures to be taken of him before a flight. This dated back two years to the time when his tutor, the ace Oswald Boelcke, had been photographed before take-off. A short time later he was dead—killed in a midair collision with one of his own pupils.

At that moment the adjutant, Bodenschatz, came up to the pilots and told them the weather was improving. By 9:30 A.M. most of the mist had been cleared by an east wind. The telephone operator announced that there were British planes in the area and at 9:40 A.M. Richthofen took off at the head of a six-machine formation. One of the aircraft was piloted by Richthofen's cousin, Wolfram. It was the first time he had been up with a fighter patrol and he was under strict instructions to keep well clear of any trouble, and make for home if attacked.

Twenty-five miles away to the west, at the Royal Air Force base of Bertangles, another young pilot, 2nd Lt. Wilfred May, had been issued with similar instructions.

May was eager for action, but not so eager that he would risk disobeying his flight commander, Captain Roy Brown, even though they were old school friends.

Brown's flight had been due to take off on routine front-line patrol at 8:15 A.M. but they were delayed by the same mist that had held Richthofen back. However, by 9:30 A.M. the mist had cleared enough to fly and at 9:35 A.M. Brown led his five Sopwith Camels into the air.

As he climbed Brown wondered whether he would return. He had twelve victories and a Distinguished Service Cross to his credit. Would the number thirteen prove unlucky? His nerves—unlike those of many of his comrades—were still steady, but the constant strain of combat had resulted in a painful stomach ulcer, which he refused to have treated in a hospital.

A few minutes later a further five Camels took off. They were followed at 9:45 A.M. by another five. Now the whole of 209 Squadron was in the air, flying steadily southeast toward enemy territory and the southernmost limits of their patrol. The weather, although better than it had been earlier, was still not good. Fog and clouds hung in the air and the pilots on both sides looked forward to returning to their bases.

At 10:25 A.M. the last of the three 209 flights to take off was flying at an altitude of 12,000 feet, nearly seven miles inside the German lines. They were led by an American, Captain Le Boutillier. Suddenly, they spotted two enemy Albatros planes beneath them, heading toward the Allied lines.

Le Boutillier realized that they were probably on a

photographic mission and immediately gave the signal to attack. The leading Camel dived straight down, twin Vickers machine guns blazing. One of the Albatroses caught fire and went out of control, spiraling earthward. The other disappeared into cloud cover at 9,000 feet. Le Boutillier and the other members of his flight followed the enemy plane into the cloud but were unable to find it. After a while he signaled to the Camels to regroup and they continued their northward journey.

All this had been watched by Brown's flight. They had reached their patrol limit and, together with the second flight led by Captain Redgate, were flying back toward the Allied lines when they came across the skirmish. Brown saw the first Albatros shot down but lost sight of the action when the planes sped into the clouds.

Then two of Redgate's flight developed engine trouble and were forced to make their way back to base. Brown was now left with eight of the fifteen planes that had taken off from Bertangles. They continued to fly north-east across the river Somme, which wound through the ravaged French countryside beneath them.

By this time Richthofen was flying westward along the Somme valley. He had been joined by another squadron and Lt. Wolff, a late starter from his own group. Altogether they numbered more than twenty aircraft. It was a formidable force.

The damp mist still hung in the air as the distance narrowed between the opposing aircraft. But, although their lines crossed, the planes were flying at different altitudes. It is unlikely that one side would have seen the

other had it not been for the intervention of two completely separate aircraft.

These were Allied RE8s from No. 3 Squadron, flying
on a photo reconnaissance mission at approximately
7,000 feet over the German lines at Hamel.

They were oblivious of the German planes massed
overhead. But Richthofen's pilots had seen them and
four tri-planes dived down into the attack. The RE8
crews were taken completely by surprise, so much so
that Lt. F. E. Banks, one of the observers, dropped his
camera plates. He recovered quickly, grabbed his machine gun and swung it round, firing about 200 rounds at
pointblank range. Meanwhile the pilot, Lt. T. L.
Simpson, skillfully banking and turning his plane to give
the gunner maximum advantage, made for the safety of a
cloud.

The Fokkers then concentrated on the second RE8,
piloted by Lt. S. G. Garrett. His observer, Lt. A. V.
Barrow, was determined to shoot at least one of the
Germans down. He was delighted when, after firing a
long burst into a plane right on their tail, it turned over
and fell rapidly. He also managed to send splinters flying
from another before his pilot followed the first RE8 into
the cloud. There they remained until it appeared safe
enough to emerge and continue their reconnaissance.

The German pilots realized there was little chance now
of finding them, so they flew back to rejoin the main
formation. But by this time the wind had carried them
well over the Allied lines and already a barrage of
anti-aircraft fire was bursting around them.

High above, Captain Brown's attention was attracted

by the characteristic puffs of white smoke. Looking over the side of his cockpit he saw three Fokker tri-planes racing for the cover of a larger group. Immediately he signaled to May, flying on the outside left, to break away and climb. Then he wobbled his wings—the signal for attack.

The Camels tore first into the tri-planes that had attacked the RE8s. Richthofen and the others from the main group sped to their rescue. But it was too late for one of the Fokkers, which was already plunging toward the ground. Then they caught up and fell upon the Allied aircraft in a shuddering and deafening frenzy of bullets and screaming engines.

All semblance of discipline was gone as the planes spun, dived and shot at each other. The Allied aircraft were outnumbered by two to one. Lt. W. J. Mackenzie was the first to drop out. He had a bullet in his back, but, despite the severity of the injury, managed to shoot a German plane down before struggling back to Bertangles.

Suddenly the hard-pressed Camels were joined by the five members of Captain Le Boutillier's flight. They had been on their way back to base when they came across the melee. Now the odds were slightly better, even though there were still eighteen German planes to twelve. The battle raged on.

Far above Wilfred May circled impatiently, watching the fray beneath him with mounting frustration. He longed to join in, but was sufficiently impressed with Brown's authority not to do so. At one point an enemy aircraft flew right under him. May left it alone. But then another plane appeared and he was unable to resist the temptation to attack it. By a coincidence the pilot of this particular plane was Wolfram von Richthofen, Richthofen's cousin. He—like May—was also obeying orders and keeping out of the fighting.

Young Wolfram was so fascinated by the tangle of aircraft beneath him that he was completely unaware of May until the Camel was practically on top of him. May bore down on his hapless opponent, guns blazing. Wolfram panicked and threw his plane into a steep dive—right into the center of the fray. Then, realizing that he was in even greater danger from the planes surrounding him, he managed to break through and sped off for Cappy as fast as he could.

In his enthusiasm May had followed Wolfram into the battle. None of his bullets struck the fleeing Fokker and he was bitterly disappointed. However, he soon forgot his disappointment. Now he knew why Brown had ordered him to stay out of the fight. There were enemy tri-planes everywhere, all seemingly inches from his wing tips. One came headlong at him. May held steady and fired a long burst. Both planes swerved and when May looked round he thought he saw the tri-plane falling out of control. Then, in his frantic attempts to avoid being struck by machine-gun fire, May went into a tight vertical turn. As he did so he held his guns open in the vain hope that another German plane would fly across his sights.

But none did. And then the inevitable happened. First one gun jammed, quickly followed by the second. May was utterly defenseless. He knew he had to get away.

Somehow he managed to fall through the confusion into clear skies. Then he leveled out and pointed his plane back in the direction of Bertangles.

Once or twice he glanced behind him. Nothing appeared to be following and—feeling immensely relieved —he settled back in his seat trying to think of some way in which he could explain his disobedience to Brown.

But he was being watched—watched by the pilot of a red tri-plane that had been circling on the outskirts of the melee. The pilot hesitated a moment, made up his mind, and streaked after the Camel. Manfred von Richthofen, the Red Baron, was about to claim his eighty-first victim.

He soon began to gain on May, and when he had him within range, opened fire. Tracer bullets cracked and arced through the stays on the Camel's wings. May went rigid with surprise and jerked round to see his pursuer.

"Had I known it was Richthofen," he said later, "I should probably have passed out on the spot."

Knowing that his only chance lay in rapid maneuvering, May flung his plane into a series of twists and turns in a desperate effort to avoid the death-spitting guns behind him. But no matter what he did, the red plane followed his every move. May was bathed in sweat. He found it difficult to keep a tight grip on the controls and prepared himself for the worst.

But help was at hand. Brown, who had managed to throw off two tri-planes on the periphery of the main battle, was flying back into the center again when he saw May's plane dropping awkwardly toward the ground.

He was annoyed that May should be that close to the

enemy planes, but his anger was tempered with relief as he saw him level out and fly away from the battle area. He was about to rejoin the mad whirl of fighting aircraft when he noticed a red tri-plane racing down in obvious pursuit of his friend.

Brown went into a long deep dive after the Fokker. He could see that May was already trying to take evasive action, but he knew it would be only a few minutes before the inexperienced youngster was shot out of the sky.

May had almost given up. He tried every trick he knew but the red plane was still behind him. Brown was closing fast. By this time all three planes were within 200 feet of the gound; Brown, who was still slightly higher, fired a burst into the tail of the Fokker.

Richthofen turned around. Then, according to Brown, he seemed to slump down in the cockpit. But the impression was only momentary, for Brown lost sight of both planes as he dived beneath them. When he had pulled up both the Camel and the Fokker had disappeared.

They were moving along the right bank of the Somme. May dodged, twisted and turned, but he still could not shake off his relentless pursuer. By now they were inside Allied lines, clipping tree tops over territory held by Anzacs, the Australian and New Zealand infantry.

May followed a bend in the river and, as he pulled his Camel up to clear a ridge, Richthofen cut inside, his guns firing continuously. This, thought May, was the end. He looked down at muddy water and seriously considered ditching his plane. Rather a soaking than a bullet in the head.

But suddenly the ground beneath him erupted with rifle, machine-gun and anti-aircraft fire. The Anzacs, who had been following the flight of the two planes, were letting fly with everything they'd got. The ground fire was so intense that May seemed in as much danger as Richthofen, who was by now only one hundred yards away and closing rapidly.

The red tri-plane flew on, apparently contemptuous of the hail of bullets. Then it faltered, its flight became erratic and, weaving drunkenly from side to side, it began a 200-yard glide-down. The propeller was barely spinning when the Fokker crashed onto its belly with a splintering crunch that wrecked the undercarriage. It slithered across the ground and gradually came to rest, the nose buried ignominiously in a mangel-wurzel field. The hawk had been taken on the wing.

May could hardly believe his eyes. He looked down at the wreckage of Richthofen's plane and saw, even before the dust had settled, the first soldiers racing toward the scene. Another plane appeared. It was Brown. May was exhausted and confused. He had no idea where he was and gratefully followed Brown's lead back to the base.

Within minutes of the crash Richthofen's plane was surrounded by excited ground troops. Apart from the undercarriage, and the fuel and oil tanks, which were ripped apart, the damage sustained was not great. Inside the cockpit Richthofen was held fast by his safety harness; his jaw and nose were broken, smashed bloodily against the machine-gun butts. His fur flying cap had fallen on to the ground. Someone picked it up. Richthofen was unstrapped, lifted out and laid on the ground. He was dead.

The soldiers looked in silence at the blood-stained body at their feet. After a few moments his suit was searched for identification papers. Only when they were found did those gathered around the plane realize the momentous outcome of the aerial drama.

A great shout went up. Even more soldiers arrived and within minutes the Fokker had been stripped almost clean by the souvenir hunters. And it was not only the plane. Before the body was removed it, too, was plundered. Personal items—a silk scarf and a handkerchief—were taken before anyone in authority arrived to prevent it.

The whole episode had been observed by horror-struck Germans, watching through telescopes from their own lines. They opened fire, sending a barrage of shells around the crashed—and by now looted—plane. The Allied soldiers scurried for cover.

Richthofen's body was taken to a temporary field hospital, where an autopsy showed he had been killed by a single bullet. The bullet had penetrated his chest on the right-hand side and emerged two inches higher on the left.

But whose bullet? Was it Brown who had sent the Red Baron to his death or was it Australian ground fire?

Brown's report of the incident read:

(1) At 10:35 a.m. I observed two Albatros burst into flames and crash.

(2) Dived on large formation of 15–20 Scouts, D 5s and Fokker tri-planes, two of which got on my tail and I came out. Went back again and dived on pure red tri-plane which was firing on Lt. May. I got a long burst into him and he went down vertical and was observed to crash by Lt. Mellersh and Lt. May. I fired on two more but did not get them.

The Royal Air Force, not unnaturally, claimed the victory for their man. But the Australians were just as adamant that the honor belonged to them. A report from the 5th Division stated:

Airman shot down by 53rd Battery AFA this morning was famous Baron von Richtofen. [Their spelling mistake.]

The next day, April 22, Richthofen was buried with full military honors at the Bertangles village church. His funeral cortege was escorted by a procession of Allied officers, soldiers from the ranks and local people. When the service had been read, and the coffin lowered into the ground, a three-volley salute from a dozen rifles sounded over the flower-strewn grave.

Among the many wreaths was one from the Australian 5th Division. On the card attached to it were the simple words, "To our gallant and worthy foe."

Today it may seem strange that they should want to

acknowledge their enemy in this way. But during the First World War battle was regarded as an affair of honor. The combatants may have been ordered to kill one another but they did it with a kind of gentlemanly understanding. Many, particularly the officers, felt themselves guided by the same principles of chivalry and fair play so admired by the knights of old.

And no single group felt this more keenly than the pilots—on both sides. Manfred von Richthofen had shot down eighty aircraft, killing seventy-seven men in twenty months. But his enemies still regarded him as a gentleman and, as the card on the wreath stated, a "gallant and worthy foe."

The Boy Manfred

In 1892 Albrecht Baron von Richthofen was stationed with his cavalry regiment in Breslau, a small town situated in what was then the north German province of Silesia. Here, on May 2, his wife, Kunigunde, gave birth to a son. He was named Manfred Albrecht.

Manfred was not the Richthofens' first child—they already had a two-year-old daughter—nor was he to be their only son. However, he was destined to become the most famous man in Germany by the time he was twenty-four and was to be mourned by millions when he died.

The Richthofens had been farmers and landowners for generations. But Manfred's father, Albrecht, broke with tradition by becoming a professional soldier. He was utterly dedicated; an ambitious and single-minded man who would doubtless have attained high rank had not a brave—but impulsive—act wrecked his career when he was still only a captain.

One icy winter he had been taking part in some particularly rigorous maneuvers on the banks of a river when three soldiers ahead of him slipped, and fell into the rushing torrent. Without a moment's hesitation Richthofen plunged in after them. He emerged shivering violently from the beginnings of a severe chill.

He tried to ignore this chill but it became worse. Complications developed, his ears were affected and soon the dashing cavalry captain was deaf. An army medical board pronounced him unfit for further active service. He was promoted to major and compulsorily pensioned off.

Quietly nursing whatever bitterness he must have felt, Albrecht von Richthofen said good-bye to the soldiering life he had prized so highly, packed his bags and retired with his wife and children to the family estate at Schweidnitz.

He had already decided that Manfred—as was the tradition with Prussian first-born sons—should follow him in a military career. Now that he himself could no longer serve the Fatherland, that determination grew fiercer.

Manfred was nearly nine years old when he went to live at Schweidnitz. He was a robust, healthy boy, with a passion for climbing the highest trees. The servants were horrified, but not so his parents who believed that children should be allowed to express themselves. And if that meant falling out of a tree or off a horse—so much the better. It was all very character forming.

But while being allowed this freedom, Manfred was, at the same time, never allowed to forget that he was a Prussian, a member of the German military aristocracy. Even as a small boy he was made aware of what this meant. The Prussians were an elite, dedicated to the guiding principles of discipline and duty. Duty above all. Duty to one's country and, if an officer, duty to one's men.

Manfred knew he was destined for the army. But he did not complain. Even though he obviously found discipline—whenever it was imposed on him—irritating, he would never have dreamed of questioning it. His military career, however, lay ahead. For the moment life was fun and full of new excitements—such as hunting.

A frequent visitor to the Richthofen household was Alexander von Schickfuss, brother of Manfred's mother. He was a skilled hunter who traveled the world in search of big game. His own house was full of trophies, as well as every kind of gun, and it was through him that Manfred first developed the love of hunting that was to stand him in such good stead in the years to come.

There was plenty to hunt in the forests around Schweidnitz and, with an air gun given to him by his father, the young Manfred stalked through the trees in search of squirrels and other small animals. His early expeditions were not particularly successful. Once, while on a holiday visit to his grandmother's house, Manfred had spent a fruitless morning hunting. He was determined not to return empty-handed. But he could find nothing and started back with mounting frustration. On the way he passed a coop containing some tame ducks. Without further ado Manfred flushed them out and into the air. He then unslung his gun, shot three and bore their tail feathers home in triumph.

On being asked where he had found his trophies, Manfred hesitated for just a moment before confessing. His mother was furious and began to scold him. But she was stopped by his grandmother, who said she should be pleased that her son had the courage to admit he had done wrong.

After that Manfred confined himself to wild game and, with practice, he soon became an expert hunter and marksman. There was nothing he enjoyed more than stalking an animal through the undergrowth before bringing it down with a well-placed bullet.

When he was eleven years old Manfred's parents decided it was time for his military career to begin. Up until then he had been educated first at home and then at the local school in Schweidnitz. He did not relish the prospect of going away but accepted it philosophically.

"I was not particularly eager to become a cadet," he said later, "but my father wished it, and I was not consulted."

His induction began in 1903 at the German Military School of Wahlstatt in Berlin. The school had once been a monastery. Life for Manfred and his companions was almost as Spartan as it had been for the former inhabitants. Their day began just after first light. Before breakfast—a frugal meal—the cadets had to exercise with weights and clubs. After that they settled down to their daily routine of intensive study and rigorous sessions in the gymnasium. This went on until the early evening, when they staggered back to bed and fell into an exhausted sleep.

Manfred hated Wahlstatt's oppressive atmosphere. Even though he longed to be back at Schweidnitz, he knew he had to endure it for the sake of his parents. He was not interested in what he was being taught and had little respect for those teaching it. But, in order to avoid expulsion, he had to do some work. So, he resolved to do just enough to pass—and no more.

Outside the classroom Manfred spent most of his time in the gymnasium. He was a natural performer on the parallel bars and vaulting horse and could shin up a rope faster than any of his fellow pupils. His obvious ability and enthusiasm won him the praise of his teachers, who had previously thought him a rather dull boy. It also brought him several prizes.

But this enthusiasm was curbed when he fell and injured his knee. The injury was serious enough to warrant an operation but it was not long before Manfred was on his feet again. He soon regained his athletic prowess but his scholastic achievements remained merely average.

As his first term drew to a close, Manfred looked

forward excitedly to going home. Once back with his family, he quickly forgot Wahlstatt and reveled in the pleasure of a summer of Schweidnitz.

A short while before he was due to return to Wahlstatt, Manfred displayed some of the courage so admired by his grandmother. He decided to be a ghost, apparently that of a man who had hung himself from a rafter, which was supposed to haunt the upper quarters of the house at Schweidnitz. No one had ever seen it but none of the servants would dare venture near the attic.

Manfred was made of sterner stuff. He persuaded one of the servants to show him the exact spot where the man had died, pushed his bed under it and lay there waiting for the ghost to make an appearance. With him was his brother, Lothar, two years younger, and very nervous.

Soon they fell asleep. But not for long. It was Lothar who woke first. He sat bolt upright listening. What was that sound? There it was again. Something rattling and moving across the floor. The little boy was terrified. He managed to rouse his brother. They both listened to the mysterious noise, which seemed to be coming from all around them.

Manfred was just as frightened as his brother but determined not to show it. He took up a heavy stick and moved stealthily forward. As the noise started again he raised the stick above his head. He was just about to bring it down with all his might when the lights came on.

There stood the "ghost." His mother and sister, Ilse, each armed with chestnuts that they had been rolling across the floor. Manfred had been so keen to catch the ghost that his mother had decided to test his courage with some effects of her own. She hadn't realized how close she would come to having her head broken.

Back again at Wahlstatt Manfred settled down miserably to the constant round of early rising, drill, indifferent meals and arduous study sessions. Now and then, however, he raised his spirits by performing some daredevil act—much to the annoyance of the staff and the delight of the cadets.

There was a church close to the school. One day Manfred and a friend decided to climb the steeple. They did this by hauling themselves up the lightning conductor. Luckily, nothing gave. When they reached the top Manfred marked their triumph by tying his handkerchief around the pinnacle. Ten years later while visiting Bolko, his youngest brother, by then also a Wahlstatt cadet, Manfred was able to proudly point out the still fluttering, but tattered, handkerchief.

Although Manfred never complained to his parents about Wahlstatt he looked back at his time there with little pleasure. In his autobiography, written at the height of his fame when he was twenty-five, he said:

I found it difficult to bear the strict discipline and order. I did not care very much for the instruction I received, and I was never good at learning things. I did just enough work to pass. In my opinion, it would have been wrong to do more than was necessary, so I

worked as little as possible. As a result my teachers did
not have a very high regard for me.

Naturally, the Wahlstatt staff were furious when they
read this fleeting but damning reference. Bolko was still a
cadet there when the book appeared. He felt sufficiently
embarrassed by his position to write to his brother
rebuking him. But Manfred did not recant. He had
disliked Wahlstatt. Now he was having his revenge, petty
though it might seem.

As he said, Manfred worked just hard enough to pass,
and at the age of seventeen he was accepted by the Royal
Military Academy at Lichterfelde. First, though, there
were the summer holidays. He spent them as usual,
wandering in the Schweidnitz woods with a gun under his
arm. Hunting was still his greatest pleasure.

But, like all holidays, the time passed quickly. Soon
Manfred was packing his bags, growing increasingly
depressed at the thought of Lichterfelde. He imagined it
would resemble Wahlstatt. It might even be worse!

But at the end of his first week he decided he could not
have been more wrong. Gone was the harsh discipline
and the seemingly endless list of regulations. Instead he
found himself being treated like a young gentleman, as
became a potential officer in the Kaiser's army. For the
first time in his life Manfred began to show an interest in
his studies. He became engrossed in military history and
strategy and went out of his way to learn as much as he
could.

Besides becoming well versed in the theory of military tactics, the young officers-elect were given plenty of opportunity to discover the realities of practice. At Potsdam, five miles away, lay an important military garrison. When the soldiers were sent out on field exercises they were often accompanied by a contingent from Lichterfelde. All this delighted Manfred. His earlier doubts about a soldiering career disappeared and he dedicated himself to the single ambition of becoming a great cavalry general.

While at Lichterfelde Manfred made friends with another—and somewhat more exalted—young Prussian aristocrat, Prince Friedrich Karl, Kaiser Wilhelm II's son. They spent many off-duty hours together and competed with each other in various sporting activities. The Prince nearly always won, but, as Manfred said, he deserved to because he put more effort into his training. Like Manfred, Prince Karl later became a fighter pilot. And, like Manfred, he died in the First World War—shot down on March 22, 1917.

Toward the end of 1910 Manfred left Lichterfelde. The place had made a lasting impression on him and he was genuinely sorry to go. Lichterfelde had stimulated a rapidly waning interest in a military career and convinced the young man that life was not so bad after all.

"I did not feel so isolated from the world," he said, "and I began to live more like a human being."

From Lichterfelde he was sent to the Berlin War Academy for a year. This was intended to round off his military training and teach him something of politics. Manfred was not particularly interested in politics but, as it was considered an important and necessary part of his training, he was determined to see the course through.

His perseverance paid off and he graduated from the academy in the spring of 1911. He immediately applied to join a cavalry unit, the 1st regiment of Uhlans. He was accepted, much to his own delight and the joy of his proud father.

3

The Fearless Young Cavalry Officer

The Uhlans were light combat troops used mainly for reconnaissance work. They were regarded as an elite within the German Army. Entry competition was correspondingly fierce and anyone who passed the stringent selection board considered himself immensely privileged. Manfred was no exception.

"It is the finest thing for a young soldier to be a cavalryman," he said.

He wanted to join the Uhlans partly because several of his friends and relatives were already serving with the regiment, and partly because it was stationed at Ostrowo near his beloved Schweidnitz.

He was commissioned in the autumn of 1912 and felt immeasurably proud as he donned his epaulettes. When he was addressed as lieutenant for the first time he described the feeling as "the finest I have ever experienced." For this the misery of Wahlstatt had been worth enduring.

To celebrate the occasion Manfred's father presented him with a mare called Santuzza. He could not have been more pleased. She was "the most wonderful animal, virtually indestructible but gentle as a lamb." She also displayed a talent for jumping and Manfred decided to spend the autumn months training her for competitions.

One competition, a hurdle and long-distance event, was held at Breslau, and although entering Santuzza meant loading her onto a train, Manfred decided to go ahead. But disaster struck. Just before they were due to leave he took Santuzza for a last turn around the course at the base. At the final—and highest—jump the mare's feet struck the fence and she fell heavily, pitching Manfred violently forward. He broke his collarbone and Santuzza's shoulder was badly bruised.

He did not do much better a few months later when, riding another horse in a steeplechase, he leaped over a low hedge—straight into the River Weistritz! At the weigh-in after the race Manfred, instead of being the usual two pounds lighter, was ten pounds heavier, thanks to his waterlogged clothes.

But in spite of these setbacks Manfred continued to ride and jump with great enthusiasm. He had been brought up with horses and was not going to let a few tumbles put him off. By 1913 he possessed a charger called Blume with which he entered the Imperial Cross-

Country Race, a race open only to German Army officers.

Manfred and Blume got off to a fine start and took the lead after completing the first circuit. Just as he was congratulating himself, Manfred's mount caught its foot in a rabbit hole. He was thrown off. His shoulder ached with pain but he got up immediately, climbed back into the saddle and went on to win the race. It was only afterward that he discovered he had broken his collarbone yet again.

In the summer of 1914 Manfred bought a third horse. He intended to prepare the animal for the autumn jumping and racing season. However, by the time autumn arrived, the young cavalry officer had more important things to concern him.

Throughout the spring—and indeed for several months before that—there had been rumors that war would break out in Europe. For the most part, Manfred and his fellow officers were inclined to dismiss this as mere newspaper gossip. But as the days lengthened into summer it became increasingly apparent—even to the 1st Uhlans, posted away from the mainstream of events— that something dramatic was about to happen.

One night Manfred sat drinking champagne with some friends in the officers' mess. Suddenly the door was flung open. It was Count Kospoth, the district magistrate. He was outraged. Why, he demanded, were they not getting ready for war? At this the officers laughed and one offered him a glass of champagne. He refused it angrily and told them that a guard had been mounted on all the bridges in the area, and that while they sat inside enjoying themselves, other soldiers were outside, building fortifications. He might as well have saved his breath. None of them believed him. After a few more fruitless minutes he stamped off in angry frustration.

The next day, August 1, Germany declared war on Russia. Two days later she declared war on France and invaded Belgium. On August 4, Great Britain joined in against Germany. The First World War had begun.*

Toward midnight on August 2, Manfred rode out of Ostrowo at the head of an Uhlan patrol. He had been ordered to cross the border to the Polish village of Kieltze, take up position and report back on any enemy movements in the vicinity. It was a dangerous mission. He knew that the Russians would probably regard him as nothing more than a spy. He could expect short shrift if he was unlucky enough to fall into their hands.

He knew the way by heart, having studied maps of the area dozens of times during the past year. All seemed peaceful as the horses trotted over a wooden bridge. Beneath them flowed the Prosna River. Now they were in Russian-occupied Poland. Manfred felt his senses tighten and he looked anxiously from side to side.

He had written a short letter home before leaving the garrison:

These, in great haste, may be my last lines. I greet you all sincerely. If we should not see each other again, you

*See pages 109–111 for a chronology of the main events of the war.

have my most sincere thanks for all you have done. I have no debts; indeed, I am even taking 800 marks with me. I embrace each of you. Your grateful and obedient son and brother.

Finding himself in enemy territory for the first time, Manfred wondered—as the letter suggested—whether he would see his family again. However, the patrol pressed forward without incident and they reached Kieltze as dawn broke.

The villagers seemed startled to see the soldiers but offered no resistance. Just to be on the safe side, Manfred locked the village priest in the church tower, warning him that he would be shot if the inhabitants showed the slightest sign of aggression. But the Polish villagers bore as little love for the Russians as they did for the Germans. So there was no opposition. They went stolidly about their daily business, ignoring the soldiers who occupied their church.

Manfred and his men then set about the task they had been sent to do—to observe and report on the enemy's movements. But the enemy was nowhere to be seen. Still, orders were orders and every day Manfred sent a dispatch rider back to Ostrowo with the message that all was quiet.

On the fourth day he released the priest. There seemed little point in holding him any longer. He obviously didn't pose any threat to them.

The next day he sent yet another dispatch back to

Ostrowo. His patrol was now reduced to three men, including himself. That night he went to bed trying to work out what to do next.

But his mind was made up for him. He had been asleep only a short time when he felt his shoulder being shaken. It was the sentry.

"The Cossacks are here!" he whispered urgently. Manfred leaped up, his heart pounding. The Russian Cossacks were expert horsemen and fierce fighters. He had no wish to tangle with such formidable men at the moment. They would have cut him to pieces.

Together he and the sentry raced downstairs and out into the churchyard, where the one remaining Uhlan stood waiting with their horses.

It was a dark and rainy night. The three stood still and listened. They could hear nothing. The sentry told Manfred that the Cossacks were in the street outside the church. Manfred wanted to look for himself. But first he and the two soldiers led their horses through a hole in the wall which the Uhlans had breached earlier for just such an emergency. Once they had covered what Manfred considered a safe distance—over fifty yards—he took a gun, ordered one man to guard the horses and the other to return with him.

Once in the churchyard again Manfred felt his way along the wall overlooking the street. He hoisted himself up and peered over the top. What he saw startled him. The street below was swarming with Cossacks, bearded Russian soldiers armed with swords and rifles. They were talking to the villagers and Manfred's immediate reaction was that he had been betrayed. He wished he'd

dealt more firmly with the people of Kieltze—
particularly the priest.

It felt strange to see the enemy for the first time. There
were about thirty of them. Far too many to risk a fight.
All he could do was watch.

After a while Manfred decided that he might be
spotted if he stayed in the churchyard. So he rejoined his
fellows and their horses and they slipped stealthily into a
wood to spend the night.

The next morning, his limbs aching and his clothes
soaked through, Manfred crept back into the churchyard
and looked over the wall again. Everything was quiet.
The Cossacks had gone. Manfred made up his mind to go
too, just in case his quarters in the church had been given
away. He was no coward, but there seemed little sense in
risking the lives both of himself and his men.

The three of them were exhausted. But there was no
choice. They mounted their horses and rode quickly back
to Ostrowo, where they were received with amazement.
There had been rumors of bloody clashes with the
Cossacks and it was assumed that Manfred and his two
remaining patrol members had been killed. These rumors
had spread so quickly that Manfred's parents had already
received visits of condolence. As he said later, "all that
was lacking was the obituary notice in the newspaper."
He was horrified at the agonies his family must have
been going through and the first thing he did was to send
them a cable assuring them he was safe. Then he went to
bed.

When he woke he found the garrison in turmoil.
Everyone had been told to pack and stand by. Manfred

hurriedly pulled on his uniform, threw his belongings together and then waited, like the rest, to hear where the regiment was being sent.

He did not know, of course, that the German High Command had ordered an almost total withdrawal from the Russian front in the east in preparation for a massive attack on France, the western front. Neither did he know that the High Command optimistically assumed that victory would be theirs within six weeks. With France out of the way, the Germans hoped then to redeploy in the east and finish off Russia. But all Richthofen knew was that at last the regiment was going to war.

Together with three other young lieutenants, Manfred boarded a commandeered train loaded with horses, men and baggage. The atmosphere in his compartment was stifling, "much too narrow for four warlike men." He therefore moved into a luggage car, put some straw on the floor, covered it with a tent cloth and settled down to continue the journey in more comfort.

As the train sped through Germany, rumor ran riot as to their final destination, but Manfred guessed they were heading toward France. At each stop the soldiers were greeted as though the war was already won. They were kissed by pretty girls, given presents of food and bedecked with garlands of flowers.

Their last stop was Busendorf, a few days' march from the Luxembourg border. Just outside the town the train halted in a long tunnel and a high-spirited youth let off his rifle. Pandemonium reigned. Thinking they were under attack, soldiers started firing their guns the whole length of the train. Bullets cracked and whined around the tunnel until calm was eventually restored by frantic officers. Luckily no one was hurt.

After the horses had recovered from the journey the column of men and equipment moved off toward Luxembourg and Belgium. Now they were no longer greeted with flowers and kisses. Instead, the inhabitants of the towns and villages they passed through looked sullen and suspicious.

On they marched. Through the heart of Luxembourg and eventually to Belgium, halting to rest at the town of Arlon, a few miles across the border. Here Manfred was given some bad news. A close friend had been killed three miles away a few days earlier. But there was no time for grief. This was war. And it was not long before he had a taste of action himself.

On August 21 Manfred and the 1st Uhlans moved to Virton. Nearby the German Fifth Army and French troops were locked in bloody battle. The air was heavy with the sound of gunfire and the cries of wounded men. The French fought bravely but were no match for the machine guns, which mowed them down like grass. They retreated into the surrounding forests.

The Germans assumed that the French would regroup under cover of the trees and Uhlan patrols were sent in to report on their movements. One such patrol was led by Manfred. He was nervous as he and his fifteen men rode down a path into the woods. But nothing happened and his confidence returned.

Suddenly a shot rang out. It came from the window of

a forester's cottage, lying almost unnoticed under the shadow of the trees. There was another shot. The Uhlans surrounded the cottage and Manfred burst in. Inside were four or five hostile-looking boys. Manfred was furious. One of his horses had been hit in the stomach and a soldier had received a hand wound, this just from boys, not even soldiers. Manfred demanded that the guilty sniper give himself up or they would all be shot. They could see he meant business and made a headlong dash through the back door. In the confusion that followed they all escaped. There was only one thing left to do, thought Manfred—set fire to the cottage.

He waited until the cottage was well and truly alight. Only when the smoke rose high among the tree tops would he move. The patrol pressed foward, deeper into the forest. They were followed by the sharp noise of splintering wood as the doomed building began to fall in on itself. That's one place the snipers won't use again, thought Manfred with grim satisfaction. He regretted the boys' escape.

He was still brooding over the incident when a shout from one of the Uhlans drew his attention to some marks on the damp ground. They were hoofprints and, from their appearance, fairly fresh. Manfred, realizing that they were probably close to the enemy, warned the patrol to be on guard. The prospect of a fight loomed. He and his Uhlans were keyed up, eager to do battle for the Fatherland.

After tracking the marks for an hour Manfred could

see they would be less protected by the shelter of trees. He advised caution, but everybody's blood was up as they looked around for the red and blue of a French uniform. It did not occur to Manfred—hungry for glory as he was—that he had been ordered only to observe the enemy. He said: "I saw myself at the head of my little troop, cutting an enemy squadron to pieces, and I was quite drunk with joyful expectation."

The patrol edged slowly forward, still following the hoof marks. Then, as the leading horseman rounded a bend into a clearing, he stopped. A barricade of felled trees lay across the path. The way ahead was completely blocked. To the left was a stream, then a field surrounded by barbed wire; beyond that stretched a line of bushes. The hoof marks ran right up to them. On the other side of the path was a cliff face towering sheer into the air. The Uhlans were trapped.

Manfred ordered his men to remain where they were and he rode up to the barricade with his orderly. It was impenetrable. There was only one thing to do. Retreat. But as he raised his hand to give the order, a rifle cracked from the bushes.

Hearing the shot, and seeing their commander's lifted arm, the rest of the patrol mistook his signal for an order to advance rather than retreat. They charged straight up the narrow path and came face to face with Manfred and his orderly riding back toward them. The bushes erupted with rifle-fire and bullets smacked relentlessly into the confused tangle of riders. The orderly's horse was hit and fell, pinning its rider underneath. Manfred managed to steer his way through the melee and raced across the clearing for the cover of the trees. He was followed by those Uhlans who managed to escape the fray. Together they galloped at full speed back down the path to the German lines.

Of the fifteen men who had trotted out so boldly after the French, only five—including Manfred—returned. As he said: "The enemy had surprised us splendidly. He had probably observed us from the beginning and, as the Frenchmen do, intended to catch us unawares, which he successfully did in this case."

He was bitter and full of self-reproach for having led his men into what he now considered such an obvious trap. However, his superiors did not seem to hold the incident against him and he was further cheered by the reappearance of his orderly, even though he was wearing only one boot. He had managed to escape the French by climbing the cliff and hiding in some bushes at the top.

A Skyward
Ambition

Manfred was bored. He had been transferred to the Signal Corps stationed near the Verdun trenches. He no longer went looking for his enemies on horseback; instead he faced them across a blighted landscape of mud and twisted trees. This way was his first experience of dugout warfare and he chafed at the inactivity.

His main job was delivering dispatches to the trenches and laying telephone wires from the command posts. Even though he had now been appointed an assistant adjutant he felt he had been degraded to a "paper shuffler." He particularly resented having to remain at least 1,600 yards behind the front lines and was jealously convinced that his brother Lothar, also a cavalry officer, was winning great glory elsewhere.

The Iron Cross (Third Class) made him feel better, despite the fact that between 1913 and 1918 five and a half million men won this distinction in recognition of their efforts. It was hardly a great achievement. He went on several successful hunting trips for wild pigs. But nothing compensated for his mounting frustration. By this time he had seen enough of the war to realize that the day of the cavalry was over. Men on horseback swinging sabers could not charge the new machine guns and barbed wire. The Uhlans had been designed for fighting methods now gone forever. This was a war of huge armies, heavy artillery and correspondingly heavy casualties. Even the Uhlans' traditional role as observers had been superseded—superseded by the Imperial Air Service.

During the autumn and winter months at Verdun, Manfred often looked up when he heard the angry buzz of an aircraft. At first he regarded these frail wood, wire and fabric constructions only as an interesting diversion. But as he heard more about the valuable contribution they were making to the war effort, he regarded them more seriously.

At the time the German High Command had not yet considered using aircraft as tactical fighting weapons in their own right. Instead, they were attached to army units and flew high over enemy lines checking troop movements, photographing installations, bombing airfields and occasionally shooting down observation balloons. The pilots for the most part were from the ranks, lance-corporals or sergeants. Flying the aircraft was not considered a gentleman's occupation: the pilots were little more than chauffeurs for their passenger officer observers. And the observers were not averse to thrashing the unfortunate pilot with a cane if they thought he had "driven" badly.

Manfred began to consider the possibilities of applying for a transfer to the air service. He knew it would not be easy, but he was finding it increasingly difficult to endure the inactivity forced upon him. No matter how hard it tried, the German Army could not break past the forts at Verdun. They guarded the Paris approaches and the French were determined not to give as much as an inch. All the Germans could do was dig trenches and sit there, waiting for something to happen.

On November 2, 1914, Manfred wrote home:

For weeks the position before Verdun has not shifted fifty metres. We are camped in a burned-out village. Wedel and I live in a house in which you must hold your nose. We seldom if ever ride, as Antithesis is sick and my chestnut bay is dead. In other words: There is no action at all.

In fact, there was "no action" for Manfred for several months. He seethed with impatience. Then news came through that there was to be a major push on Verdun. At last, he thought, something to do. His spirits lifted at the pleasing prospect of distinguishing himself in battle. This time, perhaps, he might win the Iron Cross—First Class.

He busied himself going over his equipment. When his orders arrived, he found he was assigned to the Supply Corps.

It was the final straw. Manfred was so furious that he wrote immediately to his commanding officer. For many years afterward the legend persisted that he had said: "My Dear Excellency: I have not come to war to collect cheese and eggs, but for another purpose." What he actually wrote was a brief note requesting an early transfer to the air service.

There was a short anxious wait while Manfred wondered if he'd overreached himself. Then, at the end of May 1915, the reply came. He had been accepted and was to report to No. 7 Air Replacement Section (*Flieger-Ersatz-Abteilung Nr 7*) at Cologne. Manfred was almost as pleased as he'd been when first accepted by the Uhlans. At last he could contribute to the war before it was over. Flying as an observer might not be as glamorous as leading a cavalry charge. But at least it was more useful.

When he arrived at Cologne, Manfred found there were twenty-nine potential observers on the course with him. During their initial training period they were expected to log fifteen hours in the air on map reading and navigation exercises, attend lectures on military observation, and learn at least something of the workings of the aircraft itself. Before anything else, though, the instructors needed to know how their pupils would react when taken aloft for the first time.

The night before Manfred's test flight he went to bed early, nervous but excited at the prospect of sitting in a plane. The next morning, a few minutes before seven o'clock, he was driven out across the airfield to the waiting aircraft. It was an Albatros BII, a two-seater reconnaissance plane with a ceiling of 10,000 feet and a top speed of about seventy miles an hour.

Manfred climbed carefully into the cockpit in front of the pilot and lowered himself onto the wooden seat. He was about to say something when his voice was lost in the roar from the engine. He was totally unprepared for the blast of air which hit him from the rapidly revolving propeller. His safety helmet, loosely fastened, blew to one side while his jacket billowed out like a sail and his scarf disappeared altogether.

He tried passing a note to the pilot, but that too was tossed away on the air. Then the plane began to move forward. As it bumped faster and faster over the ground the noise and vibration became worse. Manfred hung on desperately, feeling thoroughly miserable. Suddenly the bouncing stopped. They were airborne.

The Albatros climbed rapidly and Manfred held his breath as he looked down. Cologne Cathedral looked small enough to close in his hand. Then he noticed that the pilot was gesticulating toward him and remembered that he was supposed to be navigating. He looked over the side again and realized he hadn't the faintest idea where they were, nor in which direction they were flying. Luckily his pilot had and they returned safely to the airfield. Manfred was so thrilled with his first flight that he wanted to go up again straight away. But the other trainees were waiting for their turn and he had to curb his impatience.

He took his training seriously and was the first to finish at Cologne. From there, on June 10, 1915, he was posted to Grossenhain to complete his course with No. 6 Air Replacement Section.

After two more weeks Manfred's training was over and he was sent as a qualified observer to a holding unit on the eastern front. This especially pleased him because it was only 100 miles from his home. He was attached to the 69th Squadron the day after arriving and began his reconnaissance duties.

His squadron was under the overall authority of General von Mackensen, commander of a combined German and Austrian force, believed to be the largest army ever led by one man. Mackensen had driven the Russians out of Poland and Hungary and was forcing them further back into their own territory. Every day Manfred flew over the retreating enemy, noted their position and reported back. By helping combat the so-called "Slav menace" he at last felt that he was doing something positive for his country.

By this stage in the war some officers were also learning to fly. Manfred's first pilot, Georg Zeumer, was one such man. He was undoubtedly a brilliant aviator but the fact that he suffered from incurable tuberculosis made him take suicidal risks. He and Manfred argued fiercely the whole time. From the start they made an ill-matched team. And, much as they respected each other's abilities, they soon agreed to part.

Manfred's next pilot was also an officer, Count Erich Graf von Holck, a well-known German motor-racing enthusiast with a reputation for sportsmanship and daring. The two men developed an instant liking for one another and—with Holck's little dog crouched at their feet—flew a great many successful missions. One flight, however, almost proved a disaster.

Early in August they took off in the direction of Brest-Litovsk. They had received no orders for such a flight but were determined to see something more of the Russian troops in full retreat. It was an awesome sight: long, straggling lines of soldiers, horsemen and artillery stretched beneath them. Fires blazed at every point as the Russians tried to destroy each town, village and farm they passed. They were determined that nothing should be left for the advancing Germans.

Manfred and Holck were so fascinated by the devastation spread out in all directions that they did not notice they were flying straight toward a gigantic pillar of smoke. The smoke rose more than 6,000 feet, 1,500 feet higher than their plane. Down below was the city of Wicznice, aflame from end to end. Holck hesitated only a moment before deciding to fly into the pillar. To go around would take too long. He signaled his intention to Manfred who, while he did not share his comrade's love of danger, had sufficient confidence in his ability to carry them safely through.

Seconds later he realized his confidence had been misplaced. Neither of them knew enough about aeronautics to appreciate the effect that the upward thrusting hot air would have on their tiny plane. As soon as they hit the smoke it filled their lungs and they began to choke. The plane swayed violently, and went into a spin, falling rapidly. Manfred, fighting his rising panic, struggled to keep a hold. Now and then he caught a glimpse of Holck's face, tense behind the controls, trying desperately to level out. At 1,500 feet they emerged from the smoke over a sea of angry flame. Manfred had almost given up hope. Then he felt new life surge through the plane as the spluttering engine resumed its normal steady beat. Holck grinned cheerily and they headed toward clearer skies.

Now all either of them wanted was to return to their own lines. Suddenly the engine began to misfire again. It lost power rapidly. Russian troops down below, hearing the noise of a failing engine and recognizing one of the hated German planes, immediately opened up with machine guns and rifles. Bullets whistled all around them, glancing off the struts and tearing holes in the wings. Several hit the engine and it gave out altogether. Now all Holck could do was put the plane into a long, low glide and pray that they could reach their own ground before

7. Above: *Manfred von Richthofen brings his Fokker DR-1 tri-plane down for a perfect landing after making a routine patrol.*

8. Below: *Hermann Goering (right) was to become famous as the leader of Hitler's Luftwaffe in the Second World War. But during the First World War he was a fighter pilot and was, in fact, the last commanding officer of JG 1. In the center is Anthony Fokker, the brilliant young Dutch engineer. The other is Bruno Loerzer, Goering's closest friend.*

9. Left: *Manfred von Richthofen with his pet dog, a Great Dane called Moritz. The dog's ears were clipped after he had lost the tip of one when he strayed too close to a spinning propeller.*

10. Above: *Manfred von Richthofen (center), with four of his fellow pilots. Left to right: Sebastian Festner, Karl Schaefer, his brother Lothar, and Kurt Wolff.*

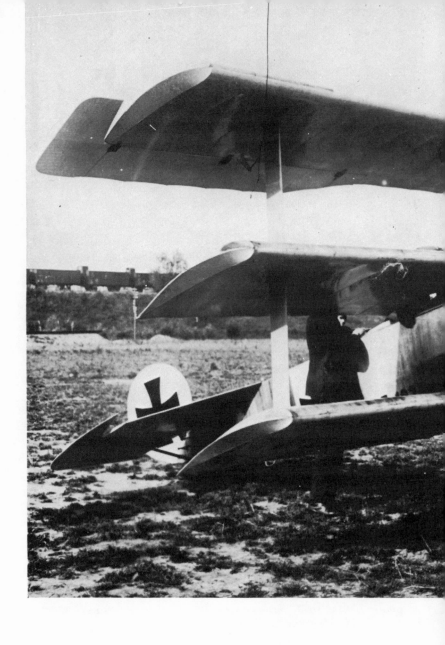

11. A Fokker DR-1 tri-plane, one of the first two to reach the western front. This one—with a face painted on the engine cowling—was flown by Werner Voss; the other by Manfred von Richthofen.

12. *Manfred von Richthofen presents members of Jasta 2 to General von Ludendorff, the German Army's Quartermaster General, during an inspection visit at Marcke airfield.*

13. *One of the last photographs taken of Manfred von Richthofen (right).*

14. Above: *This is the last time that Manfred von Richthofen was seen alive. When he realized that this picture was being taken he was furious. He believed that it would bring him bad luck. He may have been right—little more than an hour later he was shot down and killed.*
15. Below: *Within minutes of crashing, Manfred von Richthofen's famous red aircraft was stripped by souvenir hunters, eager for some memento of the Red Baron's end. There was not much left for later inspection.*

crashing. They skimmed over a forest, Holck managing to hold the nose just above the tree tips. Then he spotted a meadow and set the plane down, its undercarriage carving a deep channel in the soft earth.

Neither of them was hurt and they leaped out of the plane, which leaned drunkenly over, one wing torn off in the crash. As they landed, Manfred recognized an abandoned artillery installation that he had reported as a fortified Russian position only the day before.

They knew they would be given short shrift if taken by the enemy and raced for the cover of the trees. Their only weapon was a pistol and six rounds of ammunition. Once they reached the woods they flung themselves into the undergrowth, their hearts pounding. They heard voices and Manfred, peering cautiously from the bushes, saw a group of soldiers shouting and running excitedly toward their wrecked plane.

But were they Russians or Germans? They came closer. Suddenly Holck gave a cry of joy, and grabbing Manfred's arm, pulled him out into the open. The soldiers were Prussian guard grenadiers. They had taken the installation at dawn.

As Manfred and Holck were telling the guards what had happened, some German staff officers rode up. They listened sympathetically to their story and then gave them two horses. It was only after a weary ride back to the base that Holck noticed that his dog was gone. It had survived the crash, but in the ensuing confusion had followed the other troops. The Count was inconsolable and mourned the loss of his pet for days.

This particular incident was the last time the two men flew together. Shortly after returning they were ordered to different squadrons on the western front. The German High Command was, by now, confident that the east could be contained. The west, however, was not proving so easy. And all the men who could be spared were needed to help try and break the military impasse.

5

First Blood

Manfred arrived in Brussels on August 21, 1915. He was astonished to be greeted at the railway station by none other than Georg Zeumer, his first pilot. Neither felt any lasting bitterness following their breakup in Russia and now they were to work together again.

The unit Manfred was joining—and to which Zeumer already belonged—was based near Ostend. It was still highly secret, known only as the "Carrier Pigeon Detachment." Its real name, however, was *Brieftauben-Abteilung-Ostende*, or BAO for short. The function of this new unit was long-range bombing and, as they journeyed to Ostend, Zeumer told Manfred about the planes they would be flying. Before long Manfred was in one, a *Grosskampfflugzeug* (large battle plane) or, as he preferred to call it, an "apple barge."

It was an apt name. The *Grosskampfflugzeug* was a huge, unwieldy plane. It was slow to respond and slow in flight. But one thing about it irritated Manfred above all else. The observer's seat was situated between the two propellers and it was impossible for Manfred to see the result his bombs caused on the ground below. This frustrated him enormously because he rather gruesomely loved watching the "delightful greyish-whitish cloud of the explosion."

On one occasion he was so eager to see what had happened that, without thinking, he signaled to Zeumer to bank the plane. As he did so he felt a violent shock rip through his left hand. He had forgotten about the propellers. He was not badly hurt, losing nothing more than the tip of his little finger. But it was enough to ground him for a week. His only consolation was the fact that he had at last been "wounded."

During the short time that he spent recovering, Manfred began thinking about aerial combat. Even though he and Zeumer flew for five or six hours a day they had never seen an enemy aircraft. Manfred wondered what would happen if they did. He was soon to find out!

On the morning of Sepember 1 they took off as usual in their apple barge. Suddenly, out of the blue, appeared a British Royal Flying Corps plane. It was a Farman on a reconnaissance flight. The pilot did not appear to have noticed the German plane and Manfred, sitting in front, signaled Zeumer to fly directly toward him. Then, with his heart pounding, he reached for a rifle, which he always kept at his feet. He had been waiting for such an opportunity.

The two planes rushed past each other about 100 yards apart and as they did so Manfred fired four times. But all his shots did was warn the British pilot of the enemy aircraft's presence. The Farman turned sharply and made for the apple barge's tail, the observer firing rapidly. Several bullets struck the plane but did no real damage. Manfred could do nothing until Zeumer had turned the clumsy plane around. They circled each other, Manfred never able to draw a direct line. He was afraid of hitting either Zeumer or the tail of his own aircraft. The Farman, being much more maneuverable, managed to keep out of danger and, after turning a few more times, made off.

Manfred was bitterly disappointed, and once they had landed he and Zeumer argued furiously, each blaming the other for their failure to bring the British plane down. However, they soon made up and flew again that afternoon. They spotted another enemy plane but this time could not get close enough to shoot.

On September 23, while Manfred sat brooding at Ostend, the French, in a determined thrust along the Champagne front, captured 150 German field guns and took 25,000 prisoners. More men were needed to prevent the Allies from advancing any further and Manfred and

Zeumer were among those immediately ordered forward.

They made several excursions in the apple barge but on one occasion Manfred flew with someone else. This was a young officer called Osteroth and they traveled in an Albatros CIII, an altogether much lighter and nimbler plane. As well as being more responsive than the apple barge the Albatros had another important difference. The observer sat behind the pilot and he was armed with a swivel-mounted machine gun.

Three miles inside the French lines they saw a Farman. Osteroth flew alongside and Manfred opened fire, surprising the pilot who had not noticed them. He managed to get off two bursts and then his gun jammed. While he worked frantically to clear it, the astonished Allied observer started firing at them. Both Manfred and Osteroth were taken aback. The Farman, too, was armed with a machine gun. Manfred at last managed to free his own gun and the two planes flew along, side by side, trading shots. This lasted for thirty seconds.

Manfred had fired a hundred rounds into the Farman when he noticed, with increasing tension and excitement, that their opponent was beginning to weave erratically. Then, to his utter delight, the Farman spiraled down toward the ground and crashed into a bomb crater.

Eager to claim recognition for his first "kill," Manfred lost no time in reporting the incident. But, to his dismay, he was blandly told that as the plane had been shot down behind enemy lines, it did not count. In short, he had been blooded, but not honored.

On October 1 he was posted again, this time to *Brieftauben-Abteilung-Metz*, the second of Germany's secret bombing units. During the train journey he met someone who was to change the course of his life.

6

A Hero's Footsteps

"Tell me, how do you manage it?" asked Manfred eagerly. The man sitting opposite him in the dining car laughed, although at the same time he was obviously embarrassed by the directness of the question. Manfred, sensing his discomfort, felt slightly awkward himself, but was determined to have an answer. "Well?" he asked.

"It's quite simple," came the reply. "I fly close to my man, aim well and then of course he falls down."

Manfred looked puzzled. "But that's just what I do. Only the planes don't fall down."

The other smiled knowingly. "Yes, my friend, but I fly a Fokker monoplane."

The man he had introduced himself to and questioned so persistently was Oswald Boelcke, a modest, unassuming young lieutenant. He was also the pride of the German Air Service, having shot down four enemy aircraft. The plane he flew to such deadly effect was a Fokker, designed by a brilliant young Dutch engineer of the same name. The Fokker was fast and highly maneuverable. But what made it know as the "Scourge" over the western front was the fact that it was fitted with a machine gun that fired *through* the propeller.

The French had been the first to hit on the idea but had been unable to perfect the technique. In an attempt to stop the pilot from shooting down his own plane, they fitted the propeller blades with steel deflector plates. Those bullets not passing the propeller when it lay in the horizontal position hit the plates and ricocheted off. Obviously this was not without risk to the plane and its occupants.

A plane equipped with these plates fell into German hands. Fokker was sent for and ordered to copy—and improve—the idea. But he went one better. Within forty-eight hours he claimed to have invented an interrupter gear, which regulated the bullet timing. The plane was handed over to Boelcke and in less than a month he had shot down three aircraft.

On their arrival at Metz, Manfred was reluctant to lose touch with Boelcke and began to spend most of his time with him. They played cards together and went for long walks in the countryside. And the whole time Manfred continued to ask questions about aviation fighting techniques.

By now he was determined to become a pilot. But this

meant leaving the front, a thing he was reluctant to do. So he persuaded Zeumer to teach him. Using an old Albatros B-type two-seater he "threw himself into the work with body and soul."

After twenty-five hours' instruction Zeumer thought him proficient enough to fly solo. And on October 10, only ten days after leaving Ostend, Manfred settled himself in the pilot's seat, started the engine, guided the plane across the field and took off—alone.

He circled, trying desperately to remember everything Zeumer had taught him. But nervous though he was, he thrilled to the power of controlling the aircraft. He swept around in a curve to the left and, using a tree as a marker, shut off the engine as instructed. The plane began its downward glide for what Manfred hoped would be a perfect landing. But he reckoned without the difference made by the weight of only one person. The plane swung from side to side as he clumsily tried to correct its movements. Eventually it hit the ground, bounced and crashed, nose down. Manfred clambered out, shaken but unhurt. The plane was wrecked.

In spite of this initial setback Manfred insisted on trying again. In two days he took off, circled and landed. He still handled the plane erratically but at least he felt properly in control. Two weeks later he successfully completed a figure-eight and was pronounced ready to enroll at flying school for further training.

The school was situated at Doberitz, a few miles west of Berlin. Manfred flew there as an observer in a large battle plane and arrived on November 15, eager to begin.

The course was more arduous than he expected and he developed a new-found respect for the much abused "chauffeur" NCOs. However, if an NCO could learn to fly, then Manfred was certain that he could. He persevered with the same single-mindedness and sense of purpose that had sustained him through his earlier military training.

He also found time to relax. Whenever the evenings were fine he would fly, accompanied by an NCO pilot, to a nearby estate where he spent the night hunting wild pigs. The pilot would take the plane back to Doberitz and return early the following day to collect him. One morning, while Manfred was waiting for him to arrive, a heavy snowstorm blew up. Visibility was rapidly cut to only a few yards and Manfred prayed that the NCO would not attempt a flight in such weather, even if it did mean a long walk back.

But he had. Straining his ears, Manfred could just hear the buzzing of an aircraft engine. It grew louder and then, through the swirling snow, he saw the plane touch down. The wheels sank and it skidded wildly before keeling over. In spite of the damage, the two men managed to take off and nurse the plane back to Doberitz, where several awkward questions were asked. After that Manfred had to forgo his pig hunting.

On Christmas Day 1915 Manfred was told he had passed his third and final examination. Now, at last, he was a fully qualified pilot, ready to take his place at the front line. But his superiors kept him waiting. Consumed with impatience he fretted away the months of January and February. There was little else to do except make countless practice flights. These increased his ability as a pilot, but did nothing to calm his burning desire to go after the enemy. Then finally, in March, when he was beginning to think that perhaps he should have remained in the cavalry after all, he received his orders. He was to report to the 2nd Fighting Squadron (*Kampfgeschwader 2*) at Verdun.

On arriving Manfred found he had been allocated an Albatros instead of the much hoped for Fokker. Concealing his disappointment, he decided to make the best of things and, while the other pilots laughed, he mounted a machine gun above the pilot's cockpit. This was an idea he copied from the French Nieuports. It enabled the pilot to fire upward as well as straight ahead. In defying convention he also offended the observer whose official job it was to shoot at the enemy.

Manfred didn't care what anyone thought. He knew his makeshift device could bring down a plane. All he needed was the opportunity to prove it. On April 26 his chance came. He was on patrol as usual when he spotted a Nieuport. The French pilot, seeing the Albatros bearing down on him, tried to make a break for his own lines.

Normally he would have been safe; all he had to do was keep ahead and the observer in the Albatros would be unable to fire. But this time things were different.

The Albatros had the advantage of height and gained quickly. When Manfred was only sixty yards from the Nieuport's tail, he squeezed the trigger. The French plane's nose lifted sharply, it turned over and began spiraling downward. Both Manfred and his observer were convinced it was a trick. They circled suspiciously, waiting for the Frenchman to straighten out. But he didn't. Down the Nieuport went, completely out of control, eventually crashing into a forest near Fort Douaumont.

Manfred's observer slapped him heartily on the shoulder. He no longer cared that it was the pilot and not he—the observer—who had fired the fatal shots. All that mattered was that an enemy plane had been brought down. But it had been brought down over Allied lines again, and, Manfred could not officially be credited. However, he wrote delightedly to his mother telling her of his victory. He felt that his much-criticized decision over the gun had been utterly vindicated.

Four days later his joy turned to sorrow. As he checked and rechecked the ground on patrol over Verdun he saw a lone Fokker attacking three French Caudrons. His first thought was to dive in and help. But a strong west wind held the Albatros back. There was nothing he could do except watch. Then, to his horror, another group of French planes appeared. The Fokker dived, spun, twisted and turned. Escape seemed hopeless and Manfred and his observer almost wept with frustration. Once again he tried to fly toward the battling aircraft. But once again the wind prevented him.

Finally the Fokker disappeared into a cloud. Manfred sighed with relief. He knew that it was virtually impossible to pursue a plane once it had cloud cover. It was only later, when he landed, that Manfred learned the grim truth. The Fokker's pilot had dived into the clouds with a bullet in his head. He was dead. The pilot's name was Count Holck, Manfred's old friend. But there was little time to mourn. Manfred flew continually.

And always he looked around, like a hunter sensing his prey, waiting for the chance to engage an enemy plane.

He still yearned for a Fokker. Eventually, after wearing his commanding officer down with repeated requests, he was given one. But these valuable aircraft were in short supply and he had to share it with another pilot, Lieutenant Reimann. They agreed that Manfred should fly it in the morning and Reimann in the afternoon. On the first day all went well, although both of them were terrified the other would damage the plane.

The next day, after an uneventful morning flight, Manfred reluctantly handed over the Fokker to Reimann. That was the last he saw of it. Night fell and Reimann had still not returned. Then reports came in of a battle between a Nieuport and a Fokker over no-man's-land (the territory between the Allied and German lines). The Fokker had last been seen making a forced landing on the French side. Everyone assumed the worst.

But later that night, much to the relief of his companions, Reimann appeared. He had set fire to his grounded aircraft, hidden in a bomb crater and crawled back to his own lines when the coast was clear.

A few days later Manfred and Reimann were given another Fokker. This time it was Manfred's turn.

He had just taken off for his third flight when the engine stalled. There was nothing he could do except crash-land in a hay field. The Fokker was completely wrecked. But Manfred suffered no injuries, except to his pride.

Tragedy and Triumph

By June 1916 the German High Command was forced to accept the unpalatable fact that they were not going to break past the Verdun forts to Paris, no matter how often—or with what force—they attacked. So they decided to pull back and concentrate once again on the eastern front.

Manfred's unit was among those ordered to Russia. On arriving at the front they found living conditions so intolerable that they all opted to remain on the train. But the Russian summer was stiflingly hot and after a few days sweltering in a sleeping car Manfred had had enough. With two friends he moved into a forest near the base, pitched a tent and lived happily under the stars. At night, with a rifle under his arm, he moved stealthily through the trees in search of game. But during the day he went after different prey.

The squadron's duties consisted mainly of bombing raids in Albatros CIIIs, and they met little opposition from the depleted and demoralized Russian air force. As well as flattening enemy installations, Manfred and his companions delighted in spraying ground troops with gunfire.

He probably killed more men in this way than he did as a fighter pilot shooting down enemy planes. But the numbers never occurred to him. Neither did it occur to him that it was a cowardly thing to do. He wrote:

It was particularly amusing to pepper the gentlemen down below with machine guns. Half-savage tribes from Asia are much more startled when fired at from above than are educated Englishmen. It is particularly interesting to shoot at hostile cavalry. An aerial attack upsets them completely. Suddenly the lot of them rush away in all directions of the compass.

But no matter how much he might have enjoyed such gruesome diversions, Manfred was still unacclaimed as a fighter pilot. This was his greatest ambition. He hungered for glory and longed to be back at the controls of a nimble Fokker.

So he was thrilled when, one hot afternoon in August, his hero Boelcke arrived. Since their last meeting Boelcke had pushed up his score of enemy aircraft to nineteen. He was now a national figure and had been allotted the task of reorganizing the Imperial Air Service into Jastas (squadrons). British and French pilots were becoming increasingly more expert, and the German High Command realized that something must be done to stem their mounting victories on the western front.

Each of the proposed Jastas was to consist of about 130 men, eighteen of whom would be officer pilots. Boelcke intended leading one himself and was on the lookout for possible candidates to join him when he visited Manfred's unit. He remembered the enthusiastic young man and, after making some inquiries regarding his background and training, asked him if he would like to go to the Somme and do "some real fighting."

Manfred could scarcely believe his luck. The next day, together with Lieutenant Boehme, the only other pilot selected by Boelcke from the 2nd Fighting Squadron, he boarded a train and once more headed toward the western front. As he left, one of his friends called after him: "Don't come back without the *Pour Le Mérite* [The Blue Max]." This was Germany's highest and greatly coveted award for gallantry.

Boelcke was determined that his personal command—Jasta 2—should become the most efficient unit in the Imperial Air Service. As soon as everyone had arrived at Lagnicourt—their new base—he began to teach them the principles of aerial warfare. The point he kept hitting home, time after time, was that if they combined the twin elements of height and surprise, the enemy was doomed. Manfred hung on every word.

By September 17 Boelcke had decided it was time his young cubs were tested. The morning dawned fine and clear and with Boelcke in the lead, Jasta 2 took off in search of the enemy. They did not have to look for long. Twenty minutes later, while still over the German lines, Boelcke spotted fourteen planes flying toward them. They were split into two groups, eight British BE2 bombers escorted by six FE2 scouts.

Boelcke signaled his pilots to climb slowly behind the enemy. Jasta 2 had not been sighted and he wanted to give the British planes time to reach their destination. By then their fuel would be low and they would face a strong headwind—as well as Jasta 2—on their return.

While Manfred and his fellow pilots stalked them high above, the British pilots and observers were intent on the ground below. Each of the BE2s was loaded with one 112-pound bomb and four 20-pounders—enough to cause considerable damage to the railway station picked out as their target. Boelcke waited until the bombs had been dropped, and then, as the British planes circled, assessing the damage, he ordered the attack.

The British had no thought for the sky above until suddenly, without warning, Jasta 2 screamed down out of the sun.

They were taken completely by surprise. Manfred chose what he thought was a Vickers fighter and closed in. When the gap had been narrowed to fifty yards he opened fire, his machine-gun bullets cracking through the crisp air. But his target was not a Vickers: it was an FE2 and Manfred was astonished when the observer returned his fire with a swivel-mounted Lewis gun. Both the pilot, 2nd Lt. L. B. F. Morris, and the observer, Lt. T. Rees, were experienced fighters, and each time Manfred had them in his sights, the FE2 rolled away, its guns blazing. Unlike Manfred's Albatros, which could only shoot forward, the FE2 was armed with front and rear guns.

Manfred decided to take evasive action and dived into a cloud. He circled, and emerged at a lower altitude. The FE2 was still close to him but seemed unaware of his presence. He maneuvered the Albatros until he flew almost directly underneath, narrowed the gap to thirty yards, eased the nose up and raked the FE2's belly with bullets. Then, to avoid a collision, he swerved to one side and straightened out. As he did so he noticed that the propeller of the FE2 had stopped spinning. He watched, fascinated, as the plane began to tumble helplessly toward the ground 11,000 feet below. Manfred then put his own plane into a dive and followed it down. At about 1,000 feet the pilot seemed to regain some control and managed to make a rough landing behind German lines.

Once he was certain the FE2 was down, Manfred's only thought was to claim the "kill." He landed impatiently, almost wrecking his own plane, leaped down and ran across to the stricken British machine. Both the pilot and the observer were still alive although riddled with bullets. The cockpit was awash with their blood and Manfred at last realized something of the real horror of war as—assisted by a group of infantry—he lifted the men out. Lt. Rees died as he was laid gently on a stretcher. Second Lt. Morris was rushed to a field medical station where he died shortly after arrival.

That night there was a celebration in the Jasta 2

mess. Besides Manfred, three other pilots—including Boelcke—had brought down enemy planes. To commemorate the occasion Boelcke presented each of them with a beer tankard. Manfred decided he would mark his subsequent victories in the same way. Like any hunter he was obsessed with trophies. He was also confident that he would shoot down many more planes. So he gave instructions to a Berlin jeweler that each time he scored a victory, he would present himself with a silver cup inscribed with the date and aircraft type.

On September 23 Manfred brought down his second "official" kill, a Martinsyde Elephant, so named because of its clumsiness. He took a damaged machine gun from the plane and sent it home. It was the first of what was to become an impressive collection of souvenirs. A week later he claimed his third victim. This time the plane, an FE2, caught fire and plunged to the ground enveloped in flames. Manfred was chastened by the grim sight and said as much in a letter to his mother: "One's heart beats faster if the opponent, whose face one has just seen, falls burning from 12,000 feet." There was little left of either the pilot or his plane when Manfred landed. All he could find in the wreckage worth keeping was a number plate.

Now that he had proved to himself—and everybody else—that he could shoot down the enemy, Manfred longed to win the Blue Max. For a pilot to be presented with this award he had to be credited with eight kills. However, as the skill of the aviators increased, and many of them soon reached this number, it was felt the award had devalued. The minimum was increased to sixteen.

Manfred was annoyed and redoubled his efforts to reach the required number.

His fourth victim, on October 7, was another bomber, a BE12. The plane was struck by 400 bullets before the pilot—with one in his head—lost control. Three days later Manfred downed a further BE12 and yet another on October 16.

His progress was watched with interest by his commanding officer. Boelcke felt justifiably proud of the achievements of his carefully trained pilots. But, at the same time, he was anxious in case any of them—including Manfred—became overconfident and then careless. As for Boelcke himself, the strain of leadership was beginning to tell. He was ordered to take some leave but refused to go.

On October 28, a cold, stormy day, Boelcke took off following reports that British scouts were in the vicinity. It was his fifth patrol since breakfast and he ached with fatigue. Manfred was one of five other pilots accompanying him.

It was not long before they sighted the enemy, two single-seater de Havillands. When the British pilots, Lt. A. G. Knight and 2nd Lt. A. E. McKay, saw the German force approaching, they decided to fight, heavily outnumbered as they were. Boelcke, followed by Boehme, pounced on Knight's plane while Manfred bore down on McKay, his guns blazing. But McKay wheeled and sent such a stream of bullets back that he was forced to bank and retreat. As he did he saw a horrifying sight. In turning, McKay's plane crossed directly across

Boelcke's path. The German ace immediately banked. As he did the tip of his plane's upper left wing brushed Boehme's undercarriage and broke away, exposing the struts. There was nothing Boelcke could do. His aircraft began to spiral earthward. After tumbling through a cloud the whole of the top wing came adrift and, watched in disbelief by the rest of the patrol, the plane smashed into the ground. Boelcke was killed instantly.

Manfred was numb with shock. He carried Boelcke's decorations at the funeral, hardly able to understand the loss. Boelcke was Germany's highest-scoring fighter pilot. The British had always considered him a worthy opponent and they dropped a laurel wreath over German lines when they heard of his death. It read: "To the memory of Captain Boelcke, our brave and chivalrous foe. From the British Flying Corps."

But there was little time to mourn. The war went on. Jasta 2 was renamed *Fagdstaffel Boelcke* by order of the Kaiser and a new commander appointed, Lt. Stephen Kirmaier. Before the end of November, he too, was dead.

Meanwhile, Manfred was still aiming to reach the magic sixteen victories he needed for the *Pour Le Mérite*. On November 9 he brought down a bomber near Lagnicourt. He landed and tramped across the fields toward the wrecked machine. It was a hot day so he took off his cap and unbuttoned his uniform jacket. By the time he reached the plane he was soaked in sweat and spattered with mud.

Several well-dressed officers were standing around the

plane and he suddenly became acutely aware of his disheveled appearance. But they greeted him cordially enough, especially one, younger than the rest, but dressed in a general's uniform. It was only later that Manfred learned he was the Duke of Saxe-Coburg-Gotha, and that the bomber he shot down was one of a force apparently attacking the Duke's headquarters. The Duke was so grateful to Manfred that he presented him with his personal medal for bravery.

On November 20 Manfred brought down two planes, an FE2 in the morning and a BE12 during the afternoon. He was delighted and ordered two more cups from the Berlin jeweler. His score now stood at ten. But even though he was to add a further seventy before he himself fell, it was his next triumph—the eleventh—that gave him the greatest sense of achievement.

At twenty-five Maj. Lanoe G. Hawker, commanding officer of No. 24 Squadron, was one of the British Royal Flying Corps' leading aces. He had nine victories to his credit and had been awarded the Victoria Cross for routing three enemy planes single-handed. This, the highest British award for gallantry, was followed by a DSO for bombing the Zeppelin hangars at Gontrode. As well as being a daring and skillful pilot he possessed a technical ability lacking in most other First World War flyers. These twin attributes made him a formidable opponent.

Shortly after one o'clock on the afternoon of November 23, 1916, Hawker was on a routine patrol over German lines. He flew a DH2, a single-seater, wood-and-canvas rear-engine aircraft, known as the "spinning incinerator." Two members of the five-man patrol dropped out after a short while with engine trouble, leaving Hawker, Capt. J. O. Andrews and Lieutenant Saundby. They flew on, their attention suddenly gripped by two Albatroses far below them.

Andrews, taking the lead, dived into the attack. But long before he was anywhere near the target, the two planes banked and sped eastward. Andrews glanced around for his companions. A chill ran through him as his eyes confronted five German planes bearing down rapidly. He circled frantically and sent a stream of bullets into one of the Germans, who was about to fire at the still unsuspecting Hawker. Startled, the pilot spun away. At that moment Andrews's engine cut out as it shook with the impact of bullets fired by another German approaching from behind. He could do nothing except drop out of the fight and try to bring his crippled machine down safely.

Saundby, however, had better luck. He managed to fire almost pointblank at another German plane, and watched with satisfaction as it fell toward the ground.

Hawker, by now aware of the danger, banked steeply, turned and flew around behind one of the Germans, rapidly firing his Lewis gun. Manfred, for it was he who piloted the German plane, took instant action and circled around behind Hawker. The English pilot then circled again and the two planes chased each other around and around until they leveled out at 3,000 feet after falling from a height of about 9,000 feet.

Hawker's plane was more responsive than the German Albatros, but Manfred's machine could climb faster. Once, when above his opponent, he was astonished to see Hawker cheerily wave at him. Manfred realized that he was facing a skilled opponent and became more cautious in his approach. But he also realized that the Englishman's plane must be low on fuel and that sooner or later he would have to make a dash for his own lines.

Suddenly Hawker broke out of the circle and performed an intricate series of loops. He fired at Manfred, several of the bullets passing uncomfortably close. Then he dived down to within 300 feet of the ground, flattened out and, zigzagging frantically from side to side, began a desperate dash home. Manfred closed on him, his eyes narrowing as he tried to draw a bead on the weaving machine.

Hawker brought his plane down even lower. Manfred held his relentless pursuit as the two planes screamed over the fields at a height of 150 feet. Then, within 1,000 yards of the British lines, Manfred's guns jammed. Fighting the frustration welling up inside him, he managed to clear them and sent a steady hail of bullets at Hawker's tail.

The Englishman's plane shuddered as the bullets tore through the frail fabric. It no longer weaved but straightened out, dipped its nose almost in a gesture of defeat and plowed into the ground with a splintering crash. During the battle Manfred had fired 900 rounds of ammunition. The one to end the fight was lodged in Hawker's brain.

This was undoubtedly Manfred's most impressive victory. He had matched his skill against an experienced and dangerous opponent and triumphed. Hawker had been acclaimed as the "English Boelcke" and Manfred felt elated as he wrote home describing the battle as "the most difficult I have had."

The Blue Max seemed a lot closer. . . .

The Red Baron

The weather became increasingly worse toward the end of 1916. Activity was severely restricted and Manfred flew on patrol sometimes only once a day. Consequently his score mounted slowly. It was not until December 11—nearly three weeks after his epic confrontation with Major Hawker—that he shot down his twelfth enemy aircraft. He was pleased—but he needed sixteen.

He fared better nine days later when, leading five Albatros planes, he attacked six DH2s from No. 29 Squadron. One fell instantly, riddled with bullets from Manfred's guns, while the rest escaped as best they could. That afternoon he brought down an FE2B. There was a slight dispute when others on patrol asserted that they, too, had hit this particular machine. But he claimed it as his victory and was credited accordingly.

Now that his score had reached fourteen, Manfred's superior officers began to watch him with special interest. The High Command information office had noted his victory over Hawker, and decided that this young aristocrat might be useful to them in the future. In order to maintain morale within the armed forces—and indeed the population as a whole—it was necessary, now and again, to produce a hero, a person whom everyone could look up to: an ideal to follow. Boelcke had filled the role admirably. Perhaps Manfred would one day.

Manfred sensed his growing importance and became quietly confident in his ability to emulate the great Boelcke. He knew that all he needed was time. So he dedicated himself to work, allowing himself little or no social life. Instead, he sat alone in his room, poring over maps, charts and flight manuals. He became reserved and aloof, taking no part in the occasional bouts of horseplay enjoyed by his fellow officers.

Therefore, when he ordered his Albatros to be painted bright red, Jasta 2 reeled with astonishment. It was a startling display of exhibitionism and seemed totally out of character. Manfred, however, was unabashed by the sensation he caused; he wanted to be recognized as a formidable opponent. It delighted him to be told later by captured enemy pilots that his distinctive machine had earned him the title of "The Red Baron."

On Christmas Day his father and brother Lothar—now also in the Air Service—visited the Lagnicourt base. On Boxing Day Lothar flew solo for the first time. The day after that, Manfred sent his fifteenth enemy plane crashing to the ground. Their father, who had been recalled as a reserve infantry major in northwest France, was immensely proud of both of them.

Fifteen official kills! Manfred thrilled with anticipation. All he needed was one more and the prized Blue Max would be his. Every day for a week he raced into the sky eagerly searching his quarry. But every day he returned disappointed.

On January 4, 1917, Flight Lt. A. S. Todd of the newly formed British Naval Air Force attacked three Albatroses. Manfred, who flew one of them, was aware instantly that they were being challenged by an infinitely more maneuverable and faster machine. It was a Sopwith Cub, forerunner of the famous Camel. But it was alone. As Todd wheeled and dived in a mad dance around Manfred's two companions, Manfred waited until he could get behind the Sopwith. He then fired a long burst and Todd and his plane fell. The Blue Max was his.

He notified the proper authorities and sat back, feeling very pleased with himself. But two or three days went by and he heard nothing. He became depressed, and full of foreboding that the minimum had been raised again. Even the news that he was to be given his own command—Jasta II—failed to make him feel better. On January 16 at last he heard. The Kaiser had graciously consented to award Lt. Manfred von Richthofen the Blue Max.

It was without doubt the happiest moment of Manfred's life. His sixteenth kill made him Germany's leading living ace. Newspapers sought him for interviews and photographs. The Fatherland had found its latest hero.

Once the initial fuss had died down, the hero had work to do. Now that he wore the Blue Max around his neck, he felt somewhat happier about leaving Jasta 2.

On January 23 he arrived at Douai to take command of Jasta II. Later the same day, while leading his new pilots through a series of practice maneuvers, he was able to give them a dramatic but nonetheless practical example of his skill by shooting his seventeenth victim down in flames.

His eighteenth followed the next day, although Manfred himself nearly came to grief during the battle. The plane he attacked was limping for its own lines full of bullets. Manfred bore down to administer the final blow when he came under fire from another British plane. By this time the observer of the first plane was also firing at him. Manfred pressed on, seemingly contemptuous of the bullets that zipped past him like angry flies. Then he heard an ominous crack; it was one of the wings of his Albatros. Praying that he could land before it broke up completely, Manfred nursed the plane down, grounding it only a few yards away from the plane he had been chasing. Both its occupants were alive and they managed to set their aircraft on fire before being taken prisoner.

Manfred returned to Douai feeling very dubious about the Albatros. He felt sure that the wing had cracked because of a structural fault, not through having been hit by a bullet. He decided to change aircraft and fly—for the time being—a Halberstadt.

He took the responsibilities of command very seriously. The men in Jasta II were driven hard; as hard as he had been driven by his mentor, Boelcke. But they respected him, learned from him, and within a relatively short time the unit became an efficient fighting force. Jasta II had no kills to its credit when Manfred arrived. Jasta 2 had more than one hundred. Now Manfred was determined to redress the balance. By the end of March he had shot down thirty-one planes; he was within reach of Boelcke's record of forty.

Earlier that month he had had a taste of his own medicine when the fuel tanks of his plane were hit during a tangle over the trenches with British scouts and bombers. He felt sick with fear as petrol squirted around the cockpit. Having seen so many of his opponents go down in a twisting ball of fire, it was the thing he dreaded above all else. He glided down, expecting any moment to be enveloped in a burst of flame. But nothing happened and he landed, safe, though considerably shaken, in a small field. Two days later he downed his twenty-sixth victim, a solitary BE2.

He continued to fly in red-painted aircraft, and as his score mounted, so did the Royal Flying Corps' determination to bring him down. The color of Manfred's machine made him an obvious target. In order to take some of the pressure off their leader, the other members of Jasta II asked if they might paint their planes red, too. Manfred agreed. But he insisted that while red could be the dominant color, each plane was also to carry some other distinguishing color, such as green, yellow or black.

The next month, April, became know to the British as "Bloody April." The Royal Flying Corps began the month with a total of 385 planes over the western front. At its close the Jastas had destroyed 151 and Germany, for the time being at any rate, ruled the sky. It was Manfred's finest hour. In twenty-seven days he brought down twenty-one planes. This orgy of destruction began on April 2 with a double victory and ended on the 29th with an astounding four kills. He now had fifty-two to his credit, comfortably exceeding the record set by Boelcke. Germany rang with praise and Manfred basked in the glory.

On the evening of April 30, a few minutes after sitting down to dinner in the officers' mess at Douai, Manfred was called to the telephone. He listened in amazement to the words of a telegram:

> I have just received the message that today you have been for the fiftieth time victor in an air battle. I heartily congratulate you upon this marvellous success with my full acknowledgement. The Fatherland looks with thankfulness upon its brave flyer. May God further preserve you.

It was signed "Wilhelm I. R., the Kaiser of Germany."

Manfred was so overwhelmed by the telegram that he could hardly believe it when, later the same evening, he received another call. The Kaiser wanted to meet him.

He recovered enough to stammer his thanks and was told to present himself at Imperial Headquarters on May 2.

Manfred's visit to Imperial Headquarters marked the start of six-weeks' leave. He had been ordered to rest, but he was given little time to relax. Once he had met Kaiser Wilhelm and been interviewed by such impressive military personages as Field Marshal von Hindenburg, Chief of the General Staff, General Ludendorff, the army's Quartermaster, and General von Hoeppner, Commander of the Air Service, he was sent on an exhausting series of morale-boosting engagements.

By now America had entered the war and the High Command felt the German people needed to be reassured that this would make no difference to their chances of winning the war. Not while there were men like Manfred von Richthofen to defend the Fatherland. The propaganda machine swung smoothly into action. Millions of postcards bearing his picture appeared all over the country; he was ordered to write his autobiography—and provided with a secretary to make the task less tedious; every day he received whole sacks full of mail, some letters containing proposals of marriage; and everywhere he went he was greeted by hysterical and adoring crowds. He was idolized by the masses and lionized by the middle and upper classes.

But within a very short time Manfred found he loathed the fame and adulation he had so longed for. He soon grew tired of not being able to walk down a street without being mobbed. He began to realize that his achievements meant little to the High Command in a military sense. Instead they measured his worth in propaganda terms. Disillusioned, he fled to his home at Schweidnitz, where he rested, worked on his book and wandered alone in the woods.

9

A Narrow
Escape

During his earlier visits to the Imperial Headquarters, Manfred had been told of a plan to change the Air Service structure. It had been felt for some time that the individual Jastas might be more effective if they were combined, four at a time, into single, highly mobile units. The first such unit was to be formed from Jasta 4, 6, 10 and 11. It would be known as JG I and he, Manfred, was to be commanding officer.

This was Richthofen's famous "Flying Circus" and it officially came into being on June 26, 1917. The HQ was at Courtrai in Belgium.

Manfred had been back at the battlefront since June 14. He returned from his leave still suffering from battle fatigue. By now he was disheartened with the way the war was progressing: he was certain it would only be a matter of time before Germany was forced to surrender.

But whatever the eventual outcome of the war he still had his duty to perform. He set about the organization of JG I with typical determination, starting with the urgent and painstaking task of selecting his subordinates. There was a great deal of detailed work to be done but Manfred still found time to fly. On July 2 he shot down his fifty-seventh victim, an RE8 reconnaissance plane.

On the morning of July 6 Manfred received a report that six British FE2s from RFC No. 20 Squadron were flying over the German lines. Manfred took off, leading a group of eight Albatroses. They soon spotted the FE2s but were held back by some vigorous machine-gun fire. It seemed to be stalemate. Then another group of German planes arrived, then another, until there were about forty of them ranged against the British machines. But help was on the way. Four Royal Navy Sopwith tri-planes dived into the attack and a great aerial free-for-all developed. Four Albatroses were shot down but the British were still hopelessly outnumbered. Two FE2s fell and the remainder made a break for their own lines.

The German planes followed in swift pursuit. Manfred was as usual piloting a bright red plane. He marked out one of the FE2s and, with his finger poised over the twin Spandau guns, flew to within 300 yards of his intended and—as he thought—his certain victim.

The FE2's observer, Lt. A. E. Woodbridge, saw the red plane bearing down on them and immediately opened fire. But the range was too great and Manfred smiled, waiting his chance. Then the pilot, Capt. D. C. Cunnell, suddenly banked the FE2, turned and flew straight toward Manfred's Albatros, guns blazing.

It was a traumatic experience, as Woodbridge later remembered: "I recall there wasn't a thing on that machine that wasn't red, and gosh, how he could fly! I opened fire with the front Lewis, and so did Cunnell with the side gun. Cunnell held the FE to her course, and so did the pilot of the all-red scout.

"Thank God my Lewis didn't jam. I kept a steady stream of lead pouring into the nose of that machine. He was firing also. I could see my tracers splashing along the barrels of his Spandaus and I knew the pilot was sitting right behind them. His lead came whistling past my head and ripping holes in the bath-tub.

"Then something happened. We could hardly have been twenty yards apart when the Albatros pointed her nose down suddenly and passed under us. Cunnell banked and turned. We saw the red plane slip into a spin. It turned over and over and round and round. It was no manoeuvre. He was completely out of control. His motor was going full on, so I figured I had at least wounded him. As his head was the only part of him that wasn't protected from my fire by his motor, I thought that was where he was hit."

Woodbridge was right. He had wounded Manfred. And he had hit him in the head. The bullet scored a four-inch-long furrow along the left side, exposing his skull.

Manfred, engulfed in waves of pain, fought to remain conscious. He could not see and for a moment he could not move. Then he managed, by making a supreme effort, to reach forward and shut off the engine.

Down the Albatros spun. Manfred's head felt wet with what he guessed was blood. Gradually his vision returned and, through a blur, he saw that the altimeter read 2,500 feet. The plane had fallen 9,500 feet. Manfred had no idea where he was but knew he had to land before he blacked out completely. He started the engine again and began a gliding descent. Then he recognized a forest. He was over the German lines.

At 150 feet he leveled out, desperately searching the shell-pitted ground below for a safe landing place. There was none. He flew east, feeling weaker every moment. The blood continued to pour from the wound in his head. Then everything started going black before his eyes and Manfred realized he had no alternative. He had to land, safe or not. Down he went, taking several poles and telephone wires with him. The Albatros bumped to a halt a few yards from a road.

His plane was quickly surrounded by infantrymen who had seen him land. Mustering the last dregs of his fast draining strength, Manfred managed to pull himself out of the cockpit. Then he fainted, falling into a clump of thorn bushes. An ambulance rushed him to a field hospital where anxious doctors anesthetized him, shaved his skull and treated the wound.

The news that Manfred had been hurt was kept from

the newspapers. The war was going badly for Germany and the last thing the High Command wanted was for the news to leak out that the country's greatest hero was hurt. It would have had a devastating effect on morale.

The Final Curtain

As the summer days dwindled into autumn it was obvious to everyone that Manfred had changed. The recurring pain from his wound forced several return visits to the hospital, each time leaving him in a state of deeper depression. Even so, he lost none of his skill as a fighter pilot and he still led JG 1 with the same iron will and strength of purpose. But gradually he became morose and introspective. He had never been a particularly gregarious person; now he was positively antisocial, preferring, it seemed, only the company of his dog, Moritz, a Great Dane he had bought in the autumn of 1915, while stationed with BAO in Belgium.

Every time he lost a friend in battle he suffered more keenly. But, above all else, he continued to wonder with growing cynicism why his masters persisted wih a war that he felt sure Germany could now never win.

These same masters sensed that all was not well with the flying ace. Morose or not, he was still an invaluable weapon in their propaganda armory. Attempts were made to persuade him to give up active service, and concentrate instead on advisory work. Manfred angrily rejected such a suggestion: "I should indeed consider myself a despicable person if, now that I have achieved fame and wear my decorations, I should consent to exist as a pensioner of my dignity and to preserve my life for the nation, while every poor fellow in the trenches—who is doing his duty equally as much as I—has to stick it out."

In December he was ordered to make a tour of German factories denouncing Communism, which was spreading through Germany from Russia in the east and fast gaining ground with war-weary workers. He did as he was told, like a true Prussian, carrying out his duty without question. But he thought the whole thing a waste of time. He also detested speaking in public.

The following month he and his brother Lothar—now a high-scoring fighter pilot in his own right—attended the Russian peace negotiations at Brest-Litovsk. The High Command was anxious to conclude a treaty with Russia as quickly as possible. They wanted to move troops to where they were now needed most—the western front. Neither Manfred nor Lothar could see why their presence was so vital. Indeed, even today, with the benefit of hindsight, it is difficult to understand why the High Command wanted them there: unless it was merely for propaganda purposes.

Once the negotiations were underway Manfred and Lothar soon found that no one—German or Russian—had much time for them. So they took the opportunity to slip away on a hunting expedition together. After this brief interlude Lothar went home to Schweidnitz. He tried to persuade his elder brother to accompany him. But Manfred didn't have the time. Instead, he visited an aircraft research station at Aldershof. The tide was turning on the western front; now the German fliers were being outpaced by the British. If the Germans were to regain the upper hand it would be through superior airplanes: that was why establishments such as Aldershof worked flat out to develop and improve the German Air Service's fighting aircraft.

The New Year, 1918, started quietly for JG I. As the weather improved there was some action, but not much. Then, in March, the situation changed dramatically. Now that a settlement with Russia seemed almost certain, the German High Command moved as many men and machines as they could muster from east to west. They planned a vast offensive, requiring three and a half million men. It was a last desperate attempt to drive the Allies back from France.

The date for the battle was set—March 21—and at 4:40 A.M. it began, with a heavy shell and bomb attack on the British positions. The result was devastating. After four hours, during which the British sustained fearful losses, the German infantry stormed the trenches, driving the enemy before them.

During the first part of the offensive JG I was held back by fog. But on March 24 they were able to fly more than one hundred sorties. However, only one kill was achieved. And that was by Manfred. It was his sixty-seventh.

Again the next day, he was the only member of JG I to bring down a plane. By now he was flying a Fokker DR-I tri-plane. This was a fast, highly maneuverable aircraft, rapidly gaining favor with the German flying aces. For the rest of March Manfred flew the Fokker to deadly effect, maintaining both his reputation—and his position—as Germany's number-one fighter pilot. By the end of the month his score stood at an incredible seventy-four.

But despite his continuing success and his apparent invincibility, Manfred began to develop a morbid fascination for death by fire. When he was interviewed by a German newspaper correspondent, he said: "Queer, but the last ten I shot down all burned. The one I got today also burned. I saw it quite well. At the beginning, it was only quite a small flame under the pilot's seat, but when the machine dived, the tail stood up in the air and I could see that the seat had been burned through.

"The flames kept on showing as the machine dashed down. It crashed on the ground with a terrible explosion—worse than I have ever witnessed before."

His seventy-fifth victory was marked by Manfred being presented with the Order of the Red Eagle (Third Class) with Crown and Swords. This was an honor hitherto accorded only to royalty, the peerage and generals. He was now so loaded with decorations that he could not wear them all at once.

Victim number seventy-six fell before Manfred's blazing guns on April 6; seventy-seven and seventy-eight the next day.

On April 20 he shot down two more. The first, a Sopwith Camel, was piloted by Major Raymond-Barker, the commanding officer of No. 3 Squadron and holder of the Military Cross. He was killed when his plane crashed in flames. But the second victim, nineteen-year-old Lt. D. Lewis, also flying a Camel, survived.

Lewis recalled the incident: "I hit the ground about four miles north-east of Villers-Bretonneux at a speed of 60 miles an hour, was thrown clear of my machine and, except for minor burns, was unhurt.

"About fifty yards from where I was, Major Barker's machine was burning fiercely, so I staggered over to him to see if it were possible to pull him out, but was beaten back by the flames.

"From the seat to the tail of my plane there was not a stitch of fabric left, it having been burned away.

"The following articles were hit by Richthofen's bullets: the compass which was directly in front of my face, my goggles where the elastic joined the frame of the glass—these went over the side—the elbow of my coat, and one bullet through the leg of my trousers.

"The rest of my flight was saved from annihilation by the timely arrival of a squadron of SE 5s. Richthofen came down to within one hundred feet of the ground and waved to me."

It was the last time that Manfred was to salute a fallen foe. Lieutenant Lewis was his eightieth victory: there were to be no more.

On the morning of April 21, 1918, Manfred took to the skies in his red airplane for the last time. In the evening his pale, stripped body lay on a hospital tent table. The medical officers about to perform the required postmortem stared silently at the dead airman for a few moments. Then they began.

Three days later Manfred's father opened the first of countless letters of condolence. It was from the Kaiser:

To my great sorrow I have just received from the Commanding General of the Air Service the report that your brave son, Rittmeister Freiherr von Richthofen, has fallen. What the youthful leader accomplished in aerial combat will never be forgotten by me, my army and the German people. I share sincerely in your sorrow. May God grant you the balm of his comfort.

Wilhelm.

Field Marshal von Hindenburg, soon to be President of the German Republic, wrote:

Sadly moved by the report that your son has given up his life for the Fatherland. I express my deepest sympathy to you and your wife. As master of the German flying force, as a model for every German man, he will live on in the memory of the German people. May this be a comfort to you in your grief.

Even in death Manfred was to prove valuable to the German war machine. Young men were urged to live up to the ideal set by this Teuton demigod, both then and in another war just twenty-one years later. During the 1930s his name was used to help rekindle German pride and nationalism. In 1933 Hermann Goering, already a power-

16. *Every time Manfred von Richthofen shot down an enemy aircraft, he took something from it as a souvenir. Here, the wall of his room is covered in serial numbers.*

17. Above: *Six officers carried Manfred von Richthofen's coffin when he was buried with full military honors by the Allies at Bertangles, France.*

18. Below: *The last salute. Three volleys are fired over Manfred von Richthofen's grave.*

19. *In November 1925 Manfred von Richthofen's remains were brought back to Germany and reinterred, with great ceremony, at the cemetery of Invaliden in Berlin.*

20. Overleaf: *Manfred von Richthofen, the highest scoring fighter pilot of the First World War. He shot down eighty aircraft before he himself was killed on April 21, 1918.*

ful figure in the Nazi party, said, in the foreword to a new edition of Manfred's memoirs:

> We will hold Manfred von Richthofen as a great symbol. His memory will help us to use all means in our power to reach our national goal of again giving Germany an air weapon equal to those of other nations, but superior to them in spirit and courageous sacrifice, as was the Jagdgeschwader Richthofen in the World War.

Goering had, in fact, been a member of JG I and was appointed its last commanding officer on July 6, 1918.

In 1925 Manfred's family brought his remains back to Germany. They wanted him buried at Schweidnitz. But the German authorities persuaded them that the Invaliden Cemetery in Berlin was a much fitter place for a man of his importance. They agreed, and on November 20 Manfred was again interred with full military honors—this time by his own people.

Today, nearly sixty years after the First World War, Richthofen's name lives on. But why? Is it because he was such a brilliant fighter pilot? There are those who argue that he was not. They point out that his brother Lothar brought down forty planes in seventy-seven days, surely a much more impressive achievement than Manfred's eighty over twenty months.

What was it that drove Manfred to shoot down enemy planes? At first it had been for fame. But once he had achieved the recognition and adulation he yearned for, he shunned it. Was it blood lust? After all, he had no qualms about machine-gunning helpless troops on the ground. Or was it merely that he regarded it as an extension of his hunting activities? He himself said: "When I have shot down an Englishman, my hunting passion is satisfied for quarter of an hour."

No one really knows the answer to any of these questions. Except perhaps the man himself—Manfred von Richthofen.

And he is dead. But the legend lives on.

Chronology of the First World War

1914

June 28—Archduke Francis Ferdinand, heir to Austria-Hungary throne, assassinated at Sarajevo.

July 28—Austria-Hungary declares war on Serbia.

August 1—Germany declares war on Russia.

August 2—Manfred von Richthofen is sent on mission to Kieltze in Poland.

August 3—Germany invades Belgium. Declares war on France.

August 4—Great Britain declares war on Germany.

August 12—Great Britain and France declare war on Austria-Hungary. The 1st Uhlans are moved to the western front.

August 16—First British Expeditionary Force lands in France.

August 23—Japan declares war on Germany.

September 3–9—Battle of the Marne. Germans driven back from Paris.

September 24–25—Battle of the Somme.

November 5—Great Britain declares war on Turkey.

1915

January 5—Turkish army defeated.

April 25—Allied troops land on Gallipoli Peninsula, Turkey.

May 22—Italy declares war on Austria.

May 31—German Zeppelins bomb London.

June—Manfred von Richthofen is transferred to No. 7 Air Replacement Section at Cologne.

June 10—Completes his air training with No 6. Air Replacement Section Grossenhain.

June (end)—Sent as qualified air observer to the eastern front, attached to 69th Squadron.

August 21—Manfred transferred to the *Brieftauben-Abteilung-Ostende* (BAO) in Belgium.

August 22—Italy declares war on Turkey.

October 1—Another transfer to *Brieftauben-Abteilung-Metz* at Metz in Germany, where he met Boelcke.

October 10—Manfred's first solo flight.

November 15—Manfred joins the flying school at Dobertiz, near Berlin.

December 25—Manfred qualifies as a pilot.

1916

March—Posted to the 2nd Fighting Squadron at Verdun.

May 31—Battle of Jutland. Naval encounter between Britain and Germany.

June—Stalemate at Verdun. 2nd Fighting Squadron transferred to Russian front.

July 1—Battle of Somme begins.

August—Manfred joins Jasta 2 under Boelcke and returns to the western front.

August 27—Rumania declares war on Germany and Austria.

August 28—Italy declares war on Germany.

September 15—British use tanks for the first time on the western front.

September 17—Jasta 2's first action. Manfred's first official "kill."

October 28—Boelcke killed in action.

November 23—German warships bombard English coast.

November 28—First German daylight bombing raid on London.

December—Manfred paints his Albatros bright red.

1917

January 16—Manfred awarded the *Pour Le Mérite*, the "Blue Max."

January 23—Manfred takes command of Jasta II at Douai.

February 1—Germany begins unrestricted submarine warfare.

March—All the planes in Jasta II are painted red.

April—Known to the British as "Bloody April."

April 6—United States of America declares war on Germany.

May 2—Manfred's visit to Imperial Headquarters to meet the Kaiser followed by a series of morale-boosting engagements. He begins work on his autobiography.

June 26—The "Red Baron's Flying Circus" is formed.

June 26—First American troops arrive in France.

July 6—Manfred wounded in the head and grounded for six weeks to recover.

October 4—British victory at Passchendaele Ridge.

October 24—Italians defeated by Austrians.

December 15—German and Russian armistice.

December—Manfred tours German factories denouncing Communism.

1918

January—Manfred attends peace negotiations at Brest-Litovsk between Germany and Russia.

March 21—Germans open offensive against Allies in France, in which Manfred and JG i take part.

March (end)—Manfred presented with the Order of the Red Eagle (Third Class) with Crown and Swords.

April 20—Manfred shoots down his 79th and 80th victims.

April 21—Red Baron killed in action.

June 9–14—German advance on western front halted.

November 11—Germany surrenders.

Index

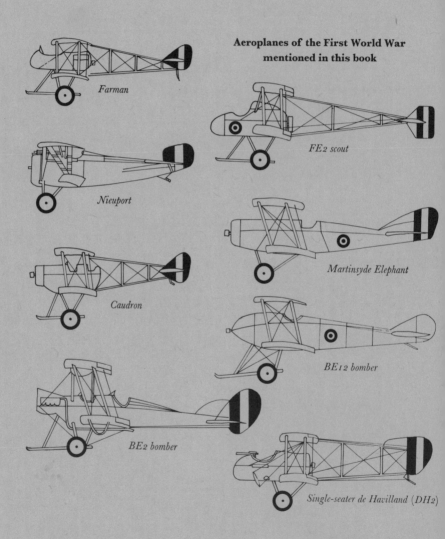

**Aeroplanes of the First World War
mentioned in this book**

Farman

FE2 scout

Nieuport

Martinsyde Elephant

Caudron

BE12 bomber

BE2 bomber

Single-seater de Havilland (DH2)